Bony
at
Bermagui

Arthur Upfield

ETT IMPRINT

Exile Bay

First published by ETT Imprint, Exile Bay in 2022

Copyright © William Upfield 2022

Compiled by Tom Thompson

ETT IMPRINT
PO Box R1906
Royal Exchange NSW 1225
Australia

ISBN 978-1-922698-42-1 (LimEd)
ISBN 978-1-922698-20-9 (paper)
ISBN 978-1-922698-21-6 (ebook)

Design by Tom Thompson

The Publisher would like to thank both William and Francesca Upfield, for their help in getting materials for this book.

CONTENTS

Arthur Upfield and his wife Ann Upfield, Bermagui 1938.

INTRODUCTION

Tom Thompson

BERMAGUI was a quiet coastal village in southern New South Wales until 1936, thanks to the visit by Zane Grey, writer and noted angler, brought it international prominence in the world of big game fishing. Later that year Grey's Australian film *White Death* was produced and his memoir of fishing the waters off Bermagui, *An American Angler in Australia* was published world-wide in 1937.

Arthur Upfield, already well-known internationally as a writer through the success of his Bony crime novels, first went to Bermagui in 1937, prompted by his only son James. Upfield quickly charmed the locals, and was made a Life Member of the Bermagui Big Game Angler's Club (BBGAC) that year: which he agreed to, "so that there will be plenty of temptation to desert the work for the fishing." He offered *His Majesty the Swordfish* to the Anglers Club, and it was published in 1938.

The Upfields were living at 'Oliver Lodge', in Kalorama, Mount Dandenong from 1935, and this first visit was revived in *A Tale of Bermagui*, written for the BBGAC's Annual Magazine, published in early 1939. Upfield was already a keen fisherman from his days at Lake Victoria in the 1920s, but spurred on by his family's enthusiasm, they were regular visitors in 1938, when he completed the 7th Bony novel, *The Mystery of Swordfish Reef*, published in Australia in 1939.

While several critics have noted that Upfield based his story on an historical Bermagui Mystery – when four men vanished without a

MURRAY VIEWS NO. 13. BERMAGUI FROM RESERVE, N.S.W.

Arthur Upfield's photograph of big game fisherman at Bermagui
South docks.

trace on October 10 1880 on Bermagui's south beach, leaving only a bullet-riddled boat; it is a typical example of the author's chasing down a story from original sources, as popular version of the tale did not appear in the Australian magazine *Famous Detective Stories* till 1947.

Arthur Upfield lived at 'Oliver Lodge', Mount Dandenong till 1946, when he moved to join Jessica Hawke at Yarra Junction. Ann Upfield stayed on at Oliver Lodge till 1963.

Upfield moved to Airey's Inlet with Hawke from 1951 to 1954, then to Bermagui South, where he lived at the Hotel Bermagui from March 23. Upfield noted in his diary for April 11 1954: "This is a lovely place.... Fishing everywhere... Nearest just across the road." They purchased land that month, and began building the house 'Tarlallin' there. He addressed the angling club at the Hotel Bermagui on April 26. The house was "renovated" with new furniture from Sydney in July, and Upfield received copies of two Bonys published in Italian by Garzanti, and *Venom House* and *Murder Must Wait* were contracted with German publisher Goldman Verlang. *Sinister Stones* appeared in the USA and *The Death of a Lake* arrived from his London publishers.

In December 1954 Upfield wrote to the Post-Master General about the poor radio reception at Bermagui only to find that 2BA ABC Bega would be in operation in early 1955. The Battling Prophet was serialised in *World's News Weekly* and the UK edition of *Cake in a Hatbox* was published in August 1955. Importantly for Upfield as a local, on 16 July 1955 he became Vice President and Treasurer of the BBGAC.

The sea air spurred Upfield to write several Bony novels in Bermagui - *The Battling Prophet, Man of Two Tribes* (which he notes in his diary as "Nearly finished" on August 23 and *Bony Buys a Woman / The Bushman Who Came Back* (noted as with his N.Y. publishers on August 29). Both the UK and US editions were published in 1957, when he promptly purchased a Daimler.

Upfield was happy to announce his love of fishing in a long article in the *Adelaide Advertiser* on May 4 1957, and in his diary noted: "Living Bermagui South... Deep Sea Fishing Favourite Sport."

Upfield's portrait from his time in Bermagui (top); E.V. Whyte's photograph of the days catch on Victoria Lake in 1924, when he worked with Upfield at nearby Albermarle station.

On May 16 1957, Upfield and his partner Jessica Hawke were guests of honour at the South Australian Hotel in Adelaide to celebrate his "biography" *Follow My Dust*, and his notes for the launch were thus: "One Spur Dick / Paroo Ted / Bob the Card / The Hangman / Snivelling Harry... The Stormbird / Bikeman Bill / The Black Bastard" – the great characters he met during his wanderings in the bush. Upfield had written an alternate autobiography at the time, *Beyond the Mirage*, which featured these characters extensively, but this manuscript remained unpublished till 2020.

With the publication of *Follow My Dust*, and with the Far West solidly in his mind, Arthur Upfield and Jessica Hawke left Bermagui South in late 1957 and purchased 3 Jasmine Street, Bowral which they named 'Albermarle', after the station in far west New South Wales where he had worked regularly in the 1920s. But Bowral is another story...

ROAD MAP
for travelling directions
see opposite page.....

SYDNEY ▣

SUTHERLAND

GOULBURN

NOWRA

CANBERRA

QUEANBEYAN

BRAIDWOOD

MORUYA

TILBA TILBA

WALLAGA LAKE

COOMA

COBARGO ● ◉ **BERMAGUI**

BEGA

EDEN

← TO MELBOURNE VIA ORBOST

1.

A TALE OF BERMAGUI

Three years ago, after a prolonged illness, with my wife and son I set out on a long holiday buoyed by the hope that somewhere along the coast of south-eastern Australia would be found a fisherman's paradise comparable with Shark's Bay, Western Australia. When I was young I fished along the Barrier Reef, but the Barrier Reef is almost as far away as Shark's Bay.

Lakes Entrance was not enticing from a big game fishing view-point. Malacoota Inlet provided only little tiddlers and but few of them. Other places were ill served with launches and accommodation. Yet others were too un-get-at-able. And on a signboard at Cobargo I read the magic word 'Bermagui'. "That's the place Zane Grey wrote about," remarked my son. "That's the place I'm looking for," I decided. And what a place! Oh, what a place! The air like wine and as cool as that in the green ferntree depths of the gully beside my mountain home!

The surf everlastingly playing its music on the sand beach before the town, and the great rocky headland to seaward which will remind one of Sirens and Andromeda, with the cloud-crowned Dromedary Mountain looking like the Pillar of Cloud guiding the Israelites to the Promised Land.

What a place! Is there any other where a man can catch fish off the jetty, off the sandbeach, off the rocks: catch fish standing up or lying down or standing on his head? If there be such a place

The Bridge to Wallace Lake, about 1935.

The wharf at Bermagui in 1937.

other than Bermagui with Bermagui's get-at-able-ness and facilities then it is not anywhere on the coast of Australia.

There is nothing difficult about Bermagui — difficulty with launch hiring, difficulty with launchmen, difficulty with accommodation, other than the damned hard difficulty of leaving it. There are at Bermagui no canny launchmen eager to take you to where the fish are not, or any such tomfoolery as is to be fought against at other fishing resorts I have visited. One of Bermagui's attractions is the teamwork evinced by the launchmen, the Anglers' Club officials, and the Hotel staff to provide contact between the angler and fish.

I regard two things, each in itself a serious business, to be accepted seriously, to be conducted seriously. They are writing a book and capturing a swordfish. A good book, like a good play, ought to reveal its characters against a brilliant background; which is why R.L.S. and Conrad leave we moderns standing at the post. I am unable to remember the names of the characters in *Typhoon*, but I remember every incident of that terrific storm.

A background brilliantly drawn cannot be achieved by an author unless and until he has become soaked, like blotting paper in ink, in the background before which he intends that his characters shall play. Two visits to Bermagui, plus the unstinted assistance of Mr. Fred Sissons, plus an inherited passion for fishing, has provided me with a background for what I think is my best mystery story to date — *The Mystery of Swordfish Reef.*

There are certain rules governing the writing of a mystery story which cannot be disregarded. The effects of a certain cause must first be placed before the reader, the cause being presented only in the last chapter. The effects must comply with the cause, but in a work of this kind cause and effect is reversed in order of presentation.

The Mystery of Swordfish Reef begins with the disappearance of a launch and three men one very calm day when there is a slight

Ann and Arthur Upfield, Bermagui 1936 (top) and 1938 (above).

mist at sea. At sea this same day are several other launches from Bermagui, a trawler working down off Bunga Head, and the R.M.S. *Orcades* which passes up the coast to Sydney. This first effect was followed by the failure of a sea and coastal search for wreckage. No wreckage is found: but a launch picks up at sea a thermos flask belonging to the Hotel and known to have been placed in the angler's lunch-basket. The next effect is the discovery of the angler's head with fish and debris in the trawler's net, and this relic provides proof that the unfortunate angler was killed by a bullet.

Napoleon Bonaparte, Inspector, C.I.B., Queensland, known to thousands both in Australia and Great Britain, is sent down to discover the cause of these remarkable effects. He states that it will be necessary for him to undertake swordfishing in order to 'test' the scene of the crime. Ah me! I fear that Upfield the angler has been at war with Upfield the mystery writer, because a critic, to whom the typescript of the yarn was submitted before being sent on to the publishers, wrote: 'When Upfield is on the swordfishing, neither the reader nor he cares a single hoot what happened to the missing angler.'

That's the worst of Bermagui. One can' t ever get away from its spell. It is a fisherman's "Shangri-La" or whatever the name of that place was in "Lost Horizon".

Arthur Upfield in the chair.

2

THE FISH THAT DANCED
ON ITS TAIL

BONY saw the triangular fin, now cutting the surface in a wide arc to come in behind the launch a hundred odd yards away. The sun glinted on the stiffly-erect, greyish-green triangle now keeping even pace with the launch, watched by three men to whom the world and all it contained for them was nothing. Thirty seconds passed before the distance between fin and launch was decreased. The fish came on the better to examine this shoal of wounded 'fish,' following a moving rock for protection. Power was epitomised by that fin: now it epitomised velocity as though it was passing through a vacuum, not water.

'He's coming! Ah, a nice fish, too. Might go three hundred pounds,' whispered Wilton, and Bony subconsciously wondered how the devil he knew how much the fish might weigh on observing only the fin. Velocity became mere speed when the fin gained position a few yards behind the bait-fish, a position it maintained.

'He's taking a bird's-eye view of the bait-fish,' Joe said. 'What about them teasers, Jack?'

'Right! Bring 'em in, Joe. This feller isn't extra hungry, and we don't want him to play the fool with 'em.'

The brightly-coloured cylinders of wood jerked forward and disappeared from Bony's range of view. He saw them go, dragged for, ward by Joe, although the focal point of his gaze had become a fixture to the fin. Then with terrific acceleration the fin came on after the bait fish.

For a split second Bony experienced pity for the fish which had been dead for hours and now was impaled on a hook. There was no swerving of the giant fin now, no hesitation. It came to within a yard of the bait-fish over which rose a grey-brown 'sword'. Bony saw an elephantine mouth take the bait-fish. There was a gentle swirl of water, but no sight of body or tail. The baitfish vanished, and the rod reel began to scream its high-pitched note.

The launch had been proceeding on a northerly course, but immediately the swordfish took the bait Joe swung the Marlin hard to port and slipped out the engine clutch, bringing the stern round to the north-east. A swordfish invariably runs with its capture to the north-east, and Joe's manoeuvre brought the angler to face that direction.

Bony had swiftly removed brakeage on the line which now was being torn away from the reel at yards per second. He became aware that the launch was stopping, that the engine-beat was different, that Wilton stood just behind him, and that Wilton's mouth was close to his neck. It seemed that it was only one part of his mind that registered all this: the other part was like a gun barrel through which he was looking to see the line running away and down into the sea.

The fingers of his left hand protected by the glove were pressing gently on the revolving reel drum, keeping the line just sufficiently taut to prevent the whizzing reel giving up line faster than the fish took it. His right hand caressed the spokes of the brake, ready to apply pressure immediately the fish stopped — if ever it would stop.

'Let him go,' Wilton breathed on Bony's neck. 'He thinks he's got a win, and he's highly delighted. He'll stop soon. He's taken three hundred yards of line. He won't want much more. There!

Careful!'

The scream of the reel abruptly ceased. Abruptly it began again, to continue for three seconds before again ceasing its high note. The ensuing silence was remarkable. The pulsations of the running engine seemed to come from a great distance, far beyond the silence pressing hard upon Bony's ears. The line was falling slackly. There was no movement on it. It entered the sea through the suds line, on one side of which the tiny chop lapped it, and on the other side of which began the flat water pavement.

'What next?' he asked, feeling that this waiting was intolerable.

'Wind in a little of the slack,' came the suggestion, and Bony put on brakeage sufficient to master the freedom of the drum. 'He's all right, down there. If you strike now you'll lose him, pull the bait-fish out of his mouth. He's down fathoms and rolling on his back like a playful kitten, just munching the bait-fish, turning it round so's it will go down his gullet head first. He'll go to market in a second when he feels the hook or the wire trace, and then he'll come up to throw it. Give him time. Get in that bit of slack. That's right. Keep it there. Now look at the line!'

Bony saw that the angle of the cord line was becoming less acute, that inch by swift inch more of it was appearing between rod tip and the water:

'He's coming up. Strike him!'

Trying desperately to remember all the careful tuition he had received, Bony's right hand left the brake and gripped the line above the reel, while his left hand raised the rod tip upwards in a flashing arc. Then with right hand again on the winder handle of the reel he wound in the slack of the line gained when the rod tip was flashed downward. He could 'feel' the weight of the fish at every sweep of the rod tip, but the slack threatened to beat his effort on the winder handle.

'Give it to the cow!' yelled Joe. 'Sock it into him!'

'That's right, Bony! Give it him quick and plenty. Careful not to put on too much brake. That's it. Ah — look at him!

Joe uttered a yell of delighted triumph, and implored the world to: 'Look at him!' But the novice was too preoccupied with the confounded reel brake and the line; and the rod and himself on the swinging chair, to accept the plea, for he was constantly raising the rod tip, and winding in slack or holding to the line above the drum. That secondary part of his brain was registering the intense enthusiasm of the launchmen and was anticipating the unbearable disappointment of losing the fish through a stupid mistake on his part.

Between three and four hundred yards away the fish was dancing on its tail, dancing on a circular 'spot-light' of foam. It was dancing with its sword thrusting towards the cobalt sky, and its form enshrouded by a rainbow-coloured mist. It appeared to dance like that for a full minute; when in fact it was a fraction of a second.

Then in a great sheet of spray, it fell forward on to the 'pavement' and was engulfed in a bath of white foam.

'I can't hold him,' Bony gasped, and Wilton, who could do nothing else but watch the fish, again forced his mind to his angler.

'Don't try. Let him go. He'll come up again. Just keep the line taut. There! He's coming up.'

Again the fish appeared, but not this time to dance. It shot out from, and above the water pavement, and fell with barely a splash. 'Now he'll fight you,' Wilton hissed. 'Brake a bit, but not too much or the line will part.'

Along the line came a succession of heavy tugs, each tug tearing line off the reel against brakeage. Abruptly the line went slack and frantically Bony wound line on to the drum which began to cascade water. Then again came the weight on the line and another series of tugs when all the wet line he had gained was lost to him.

'He's gonna breach again,' Joe shouted.

'Too right, he is,' Wilton said in agreement. 'He can't get rid of the hook down under by belching like a dog 'cos he can't swim backwards and must always go for'ards. Only in the air can he get rid of it, and that's when an angler's likely to lose him if the fish has a slack line. Get me?'

Bony nodded his head vigorously. Perspiration was running down his face, and his left forearm was beginning to be filled with lead. The fish appeared on the surface of the water, threshing it into a smother for three seconds. Then down it went and, despite brakeage, it tore fifty yards of line off the reel.

Bony was gaining confidence. He recognised that patience and correct judgment with the brake were the two essentials of success. To have struck before the psychological moment would have taken the bait fish out of the mouth of the swordfish; to have permitted the line to slacken when the fish was out of the water would have permitted it to disgorge the hook; and to have too much brakeage on the line when those terrible tugs were given would have snapped the rod or have parted the cord able to withstand a breaking strain only of eighty-eight pounds. And away down there in the depths fought a fish weighing hundreds of pounds, and a power strength much greater than its weight.

'You've got him: fast, I think,' Wilton said, loudly, triumphantly.

'You're doing all right. He won't come up again. Just take your time. Give him line when he wants it bad. Get it back on the reel when he gives you a chance. That's the ticket. You're gaining yards and losing only feet. Bring her round to starboard a bit, Joe. Bony's gonna be a Zane Grey yet.'

'Too right, he is, too ruddy right,' Joe chortled, and again one part of Bony's mind registered the extraordinary enthusiasm of men who were only looking on. His left arm now ached badly, and his face and neck were dripping sweat. But his blood was on fire and his pulses beat like Thor's great hammer. Confidence was strengthening, and for half a minute he permitted himself to rest, merely 'holding' the fish. Then up again went the rod tip, to fall once more and so permit slack line to be wound in. His knees were dripping with salt water from the wet line on the reel. His mind was bathed in the water of pure ecstasy.

'He's coming to!' cried Wilton. 'He's not far away now by the amount of line on your reel. Look! — There's the swivel. When you get the swivel near your rod tip, bring it way back for'ard' to me. Starboard a bit, Joe.'

'Starboard it is. How's she coming?' demanded Joe, meaning the fish.

'Coming in well. Leave the wheel, Joe, and bring the gaff and the ropes.'

Wilton pulled leather gloves over his amber hands, and Joe nimbly came aft with the gaff on its pole handle, and like a cat he placed gaff and ropes in readiness for use. Bony wanted to shout but was too breathless. There to the surface of the water only ten feet from the launch, rose the dorsal fin of his fish, and behind it the long back fins all erect like the 'prickles' along the back of some lizards. There was no fight left in the fish. It was drawn easily alongside the launch and Wilton grasped the wire trace with his gloved hands.

'Careful. Watch out! He's not ours yet and he might want to take another run," Wilton said. Joe laid the gaff under the torpedo-shaped body and hauled on pole and rope attached to the gaff.

Out came the pole. Joe leaned back on the gaff rope while Wilton snatched up another and leaned overside to slip a noose about the flailing tail. When he stood up his head and shoulders cascaded sea-water. He was smiling; and Joe began a chuckle that made his whiskers expand like the quills of a porcupine.

'Take it easy Bony,' he shouted. 'He's ours. Congratulations.'

Both men had to shake hands with Bony, who smiled his appreciation, and was then asked to stand aside. The rod was unshipped and put away for'ard for the moment. Then followed five minutes of hauling by the launchmen to drag the fish up and across the stern of the Marlin, where it was securely lashed.

'Ah!' breathed Wilton, when the three stood to regard the capture. 'A nice striped marlin. Two hundred and forty pounds, eh, Joe?'

Joe squinted at the fish from the sword point to tail fins. He grimaced; pursed his lips. He might have been a butcher judging the weight of a store bullock.

'Might go a bit more,' he said slowly. "E's in good nick. 'Is tail's round as a barrel. Yes, might go two hundred and forty-eight pounds.''

'Well, we'll have to get under way,' Wilton ordered. 'May be another swordie or two about here on the reef.

The gaff and ropes were stowed: Joe went back to the wheel and the Marlin continued her trolling at three knots to the hour. Bony's arms and legs ached from the exertion, but no man was ever more proud of his bride than he was of that beautiful fish, gleaming green and blue and grey. He stretched himself, yawned and rolled a cigarette whilst Wilton reset the rod, and baited the hook. Joe began to sing about a fair 'may-den' who sold her beer in gallon pots.

Overboard went the bait-fish to begin its spell of skimming the surface after the launch. Overboard went the teasers to skip and dive and dart. Wilton went for'ard to stand beside the mast, and slowly the Marlin sauntered along the pavement this day laid down above Swordfish Reef. In his angler's chair Bony relaxed and smoked. Constantly his gaze rested· on the fish, its sword protruding over one side of the launch and its tail over the other.

'Ahoy!' shouted Wilton, pointing aloft.

And there fluttering lazily at the masthead flew the coveted flag with a small white swordfish on the blue background.

Bony stood and gravely raised his old hat to it. He had never dreamed that life had in store an experience like this.

KING OF GAME FISH

Upfield's son James with the catch, Bermagui 1937.

3.

MARLIN, KING OF GAMEFISH

THE sea snarls "No, you won't!" And the river hisses "Yes, I will!"

For centuries the Pacific Ocean has thus been arguing with the Bermagui River some 250 miles south of Sydney on the long east coast of Australia. The struggle is ceaseless - the sea trying to block the river with sand, and the river maintaining a narrow channel through the sand bar deep enough for the passage of 50-foot launches.

During the short antipodean winter, the prevailing ocean current is from the cold south. Then, toward the end of September, there appears on the calm surface of a bay, a dark patch which remains a little while, disappears and reappears elsewhere. The patch is caused by a shoal of sprats, which herald the arrival of the great army of surface-feeding fish coming from the warm tropics.

The great controller of this army of fish is a tiny, seemingly helpless creature called plankton, which moves with jerky motion as it maintains itself within the boundary of a warm current. Before the main warm current comes pushing its way down the coast, there are what can be termed scout warm currents, each one covering many square miles but separated from the others by cold currents which oppose them. A warm current is not always on or close to the surface, for on a blazing hot day the temperature of the water twenty feet below is often higher than the temperature of the water nearer the sun.

Thus, during early summer there are these vast warm-water areas inhabited by the plankton, and where the plankton is, there, too, will be the tuna, the salmon and the barracuda. And where these large fish are active, there, too, will be the surface sharks and the swordfish. Elsewhere, the sea will be empty.

The type of swordfish found so far south is the marlin: the striped marlin, which is exceedingly agile; the black, which is less swift but stronger; and the blue marlin, which maintains its lovely iridescent colouring long after it has been caught. The marlin's sword is almost round and can measure up to three feet. The average weight of the fish is about 275 lbs. The sailfish is never found as far south, and the broad-bill, which has a flat and slightly serrated sword, has never been caught in these waters, although their swords have often been washed up on the beaches.

Shall we go out big-game angling? To succeed, one must be rigidly self-controlled, possess the virtue of patience under strain and have a workable imagination. Otherwise, valuable equipment may be broken or lost.

The launch and the crew of two are ready at eight o'clock. The barometer is registering 30.5, and a launch already at sea has radioed that the water temperature is 73 degrees. Bolted to the low stern is the angler's chair, pivoted to turn where desired. To the edge of the chair is bolted the butt of the heavy rod. To this is attached the great steel reel fitted with a brake to control the 900 yards of cord line which has a snapping strain of only 90 lbs. When seated, the angler has the rod between his knees, and the reel is clipped to his body harness. Thus, it cannot be pulled overboard.

To the hook is threaded a one and a half pound bonito or kingfish. This baited hook is then attached to a wire trace which, in turn, is fastened to the end of the cord line. The dead bait-fish is towed behind the moving launch about thirty feet astern, and from a boom on either side of the craft are towed imitation fish called teasers. So we have three small fish forever trying, as it seems, to reach the safety of the launch.

All is now ready for the big fish which may appear at any second or may keep the angler waiting all day and, perhaps, for several days.

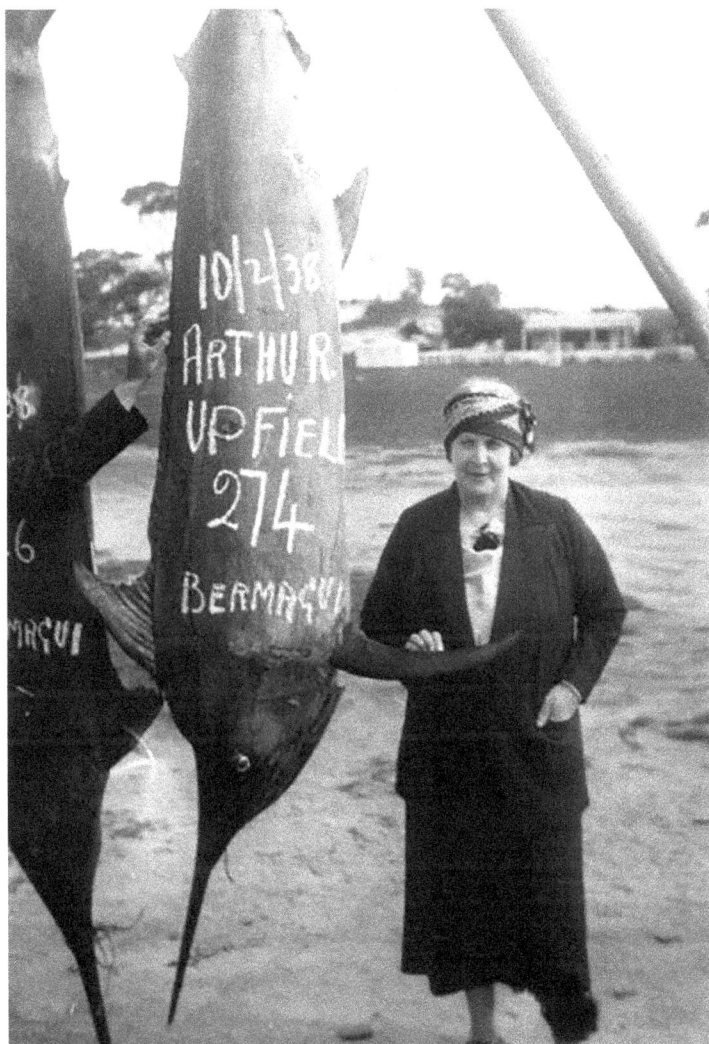

Ann Upfield, Bermagui 1938.

Zane Grey, one of the greatest of all big-game anglers, never used more than one hook and, more often than not, was satisfied with bringing only one marlin to the gaff per day. This is an unwritten law, unfortunately not always observed, that is intended to favor the fish and demands skill, patience and wisdom on the part of the angler. To use more than one hook is not unlike caging a lion before shooting it.

The wind is from the northeast and is raising a chop to meet the ground swell from the south. The air is free of spindrift and land smoke, and the water is remarkably clear and like liquid turquoise. On the port side, the coast curves in a great bay behind which is the two-thousand foot Mount Dromedary. Fourteen miles up the coast is Montague Island with its lighthouse. On its rocks bask the seals, and amid the dunes burrow the little blue penguins. To starboard is the Pacific Ocean, that part of it between Australia and New Zealand called the Tasman Sea.

We are off to fish around Montague Island. A gannet dips into a nose dive, folding its wings tightly the instant it meets the water like a dropped stone. We can count six before it reappears with a sprat in its beak. An albatross floats above the launch with unsurpassed grace, its black eyes watchful, its snowy breast and underwings reflecting vividly the blue of the sea. These are excellent signs, for were these birds not working, we might as well go home.

One launchman steers, the other keeps a lookout ahead and abeam. The angler watches his bait-fish and the teasers. It is the anticipation of battle that is the real thrill of this sport, for the angler must watch his bait-fish all day, sometimes. For several days, and often sees nothing else. Soon he feels he is the fourth fish, ever frantically trying to reach the safety of the launch, ever spurred by the threat of unseen monsters.

Suddenly, the course is altered. The launch is steered toward a patch of dark water not agitated by wind or crosscurrents, a colour patch pinned to the blue cloth of the sea by a fish shoal. As the distance decreases, we see that the patch extends to cover a square mile. Fish! By the ton. Enough fish to sink a five-thousand-ton ship. Tuna! Yellow-fin! You can see them beyond the face of the swells, all about the same size, perhaps fourteen pounds. No wonder a man can haul in tuna until he drops with exhaustion!

A placid morning and a placid sea, and then all this chaos of life and movement. Close to the launch, ignoring it, appears a long, blue-gray marlin prowed by an iron- hard, brown sword. It leaps forward on the surface like a hound straining at a leash. Before it the water is churned white by smaller fish frantically trying to evade that sword smashing down upon them, shattering some, wounding others. The marlin cannot miss. Down he goes to feed on the pieces before the fish blood attracts the sharks.

As soon as the marlin disappears, so do the yellow-fin. The sea returns to emptiness again, or so it would appear. The launch is steered in a circle with the hope of attracting the marlin by the bait-fish and the teasers. The circling continues, for part of the shoal must still be under it. Then, three yards behind the bait-fish, a fin rises. A large triangular fin with a dull white spot in its centre. A mako! A fighting shark! One second an empty sea; the next, that ugly, sinister fin is seen tracking the bait-fish. Poor bait-fish! Run … RUN!

The great fish weaves through the water, drawing ever closer. Then it angles side-ways. And up beside the bait-fish appears a grayish snout, blunt, gashed by a widening cavern, water-washed and gleaming with teeth. Amid the swirl the bait-fish vanishes and the snout sinks into the sea.

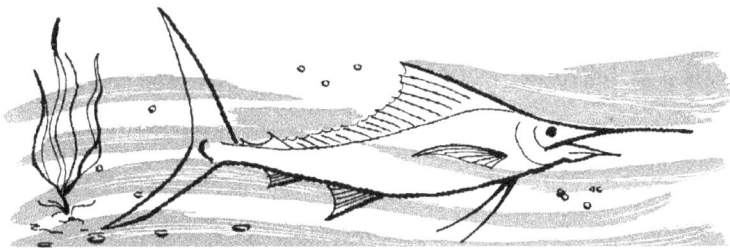

"It is a great challenge and a great thrill to land a marlin, shrewdest fighter in the sea."

Arthur Upfield, fishing for Marlin off Bermagui.

Everything seems to happen at once. The reel screams as the line is torn from it at many feet per second. The launch is stopped. The steersman waits for orders from the other man, who has stationed himself behind the angler's chair. The angler need not be patient with this monster, for what has gone into the maw will be buried there. He can feel the fish slowing up on its dash, beginning to champ on the wire trace.

The shark is hooked. Away it goes full speed. The angler can do nothing to stop it, for it probably weighs three hundred pounds and the line, remember, is only ninety pounds strong. Slowly, the angler increases the brakeage on the reel, waiting for the moment when the reel will cease its screaming.

Four hundred yards of line are buried in the sea before this happens. Then the angler begins his battle. The line is wound in to take up the slack, and the rod tip is flashed upward for the angler to get the feel of the fish. Then, down goes the rod tip, and the arc gives the line a trifle of slack which can be wound in on the reel. In this way the shark is brought slowly round to point at the angler. Now the brute is wondering what is wrong with that morsel of fish that seems to be trying to get away. What impertinence, the mako thinks. The angler can almost feel it thinking as the fingers of his left hand caress the line and his right hand manipulates the reel brake. He keeps the line taut but is ready to release brakeage at a moment's notice. Ah! The mako is surfacing. It is now getting angry. As it rises it begins to roll, feeling the line drag, testing the trace with its teeth, becoming every second more infuriated with this thing that has the audacity to fight back.

There it is! Two hundred yards away, pounding the surface to white suds. The angler is constantly raising and lowering the rod tip, gaining line, knowing he may have to lose it again soon. The shark is shaking its head like a water dog, and if the angler is not careful one of those tugs will snap his line or break his rod. The launchman is even more anxious than the angler. Everything depends on the angler's use of the reel brake and on his ability to think ahead of the shark.

Like most of us, when a shark loses its temper it stops thinking. And, provided, of course, that the angler loses neither his temper nor his patience, the shark will finally lose the battle. Had the mako continued to think, it would have wound the line around its powerful tail, jerked twice and snapped the line like cotton. That is, if it had caught the angler off guard. But it is not thinking any more. It is rushing about without plan, and every time it feels it is free it is braked hard. The minutes pass, as slowly it tires, but suddenly it flares out in rage. Its remaining strength is capable of parting the line and snapping the rod.

The angler is also having a tough time. He, too, is tiring, and perspiration is running down his face and arms. But slowly the cord on the reel drum is growing more and more as he regains it from the sea.

There is a flurry of foam a hundred yards away. A heaving mass flails at the line, which jerks the rod tip dangerously, but the angler's timing is good enough to prevent damage. The flurry disappears; the fight for line continues … until out of the sea comes the bright brass swivel joining line to wire trace.

The shark has fought every yard of line gained. Now swiftly it comes round to the port side, and the men can see it under the surface. Then, with incredible speed, it rushes toward the launch and actually tries to come aboard to attack the angler.

This was expected. The leap falls short. The shark is spent but certainly not harmless. It is played by the angler for a few minutes longer until it is safely brought alongside and stunned with an iron bar before being gaffed and brought inboard to be taken back for weighing and recording in the club's register.

A marlin! There is no mistaking its dorsal fin for it does not waggle like that of a shark. It cuts through the water clean and with purpose and is reputed to travel at more than sixty miles an hour. It is like a rapier compared with a bludgeon, a race horse with a lumbering turtle. It thinks and fights and never loses its temper. You cannot loathe a marlin as you can a shark.

It circles the launch, fades astern and comes on after the bait-fish and the teasers. The teasers are drawn inboard. The men think the fish has lost interest when suddenly its fin appears behind the bait-fish, there to maintain distance for a full mile. Then it flashes toward the bait-fish and opens an elephantine mouth prowed with a sword instead of a trunk.

After that the reel screams, and the line runs away like cotton from a reel to a bobbin. The angler watches the line on the reel dwindle and dwindle. The shrilling sound of the turning reel seems never-ending. And it does not end until more than half of the nine hundred yards are buried in the sea.

The angler must wait. What is going on in the depth of the ocean? The fish is turning the bait over and over in its toothless jaws, crunching it before swallowing it head first. A move from the angler would snatch the bait away. He must watch the angle of the line with the plane of the sea until the alteration of the angle informs him that the fish is coming up to surface. The marlin has now felt the hook. It can get rid of the hook only by disgorging it in the air. So the angler must wait until the fish comes up before making his strike by raising and lowering the rod and winding in the line.

There it is! Up from the glittering sea springs the loveliest creature in all the oceans. It appears to be dancing on its tail, the tail resting on a mound of purest snow, the utterly beautiful body enshrined in a mist of rainbow colours. It shakes its long head, with its sword thrusting at the cobalt sky in royal defiance. How long does it dance? Three seconds, perhaps four; then down it goes and off and away, eventually to come up for a second dance which does not compare with the first.

Following the last dance, the fish tears away, the line leaping after it. The brake goes on. Presently, besides the brakeage there is also the weight of the hundreds of yards of line to make the fish pause and maybe, think about this problem.

Now, the angler must watch out.

The fish attempts to wind the line around itself. If it succeeds, the drag will be off its head. The angler must fight it without pause. If the fish is given a slack line, it will wind it about its sword and snap it with a savage jerk. Now it tries another trick. It races back toward the launch and proves that the angler cannot wind in line fast enough. Water pours off the reel. Sweat pours off the angler. The steersman keeps the stern of the launch to the fish, and the angler's assistant can only prance with excitement.

Then the fish sheers away. There is much slack of line, and the thinking fish now proceeds to wind it round itself, taking a purchase on it with its powerful tail. The slack is gained by the angler who now counters the fish by leaving it sufficient slack, so that when it lashes with its tail there is no tautness of line.

Thus the fight goes on for thirty minutes … forty. The fish tries trick after trick. The angler and the launchmen know almost exactly what it is doing and what it will try to do next.

At last the marlin is brought to the gaff and hauled aboard to lie beside the mako. A blue flag is hoisted to the masthead for the sword fish and a red one for the shark, so that the club officials may be waiting at the jetty to weigh and record.

This particular marlin, which weighs 294 pounds, was conquered after 42 minutes, but more than once this angler and his boatmen have sadly regarded a broken line and cheered the fellow who got away.

Upfield with Marlin, caught off Bermagui in 1938.

4.

WITH HIS MAJESTY THE SWORDFISH

THE engine's soft-thudding beat is as regular as a healthy heart, and the ocean-going launch lumbers along at a mere three knots to the hour. The wind is from off the land, from it being absent the freshness of the sea breeze. The water mountains are far spaced by wide valleys. It is a hot morning, and the world of water and air appears utterly vacant of life.

Eight miles to the west is the coast of southern New South Wales, here dominated by the land mountain named Dromedary. The coastal sand beaches are almost out of sight and hidden by the faint blue haze. A few miles to the north is Montague Island, crowned by its white lighthouse and red-roofed buildings. Far to the south Bungah Head points a grey finger across the Tasman to New Zealand.

Aboard the launch there is no sound save that of the engine. Arthur Taylor, the launch owner and fisherman, is sitting on the cabin decking right forward. Standing within the glass-protected cabin entrance, his "mate" is steering. In one of the two swivel chairs situated astern lounges the angler, leather body harness suspended from the seat back and canvas gloves ready for use beneath the rubber cushion. He sits straddling a heavy rod, the butt of which is affixed to the seat edge with brass swivel and bolt. A great steel reel is clamped to the top side of the rod, a reel carrying nine hundred yards of cord line. The blunt tip of the rod protrudes beyond the stern rail, and from it dips the cord line to the length of wire trace to which is attached the baited hook, a two-pound salmon now skimming above the water like a small speed boat.

Either side the launch a pole protrudes to which is fastened a length of light rope drawing a brightly-coloured cylinder of wood that incessantly darts this way and that beneath the surface. These "teasers" work outside the bait-fish and a little ahead of it, and to any interested fish they and the bait appear to be a school of three small fish following the launch.

This does not seem to be a good day for swordfishing, but one ideal for dozing. The sunlight on the water is trying to the eyes of even the seasoned Taylor and his mate. In her especially rigged chair the angler's wife has succumbed, while to master the urge to sleep the angler constantly stands up and moves about. Taylor, up for'ard, is visually searching for the signs of fish, and the angler's business is to watch his trolling bait and the sea astern.

Several miles seaward are two other launches from Bermagui, their masts bare of blue or red bunting denoting a catch. A third launch is trolling between the island and the mainland. Two brown mutton birds wheel and dip below the summit of a swell, to appear hundreds of yards from where they vanished. Taylor is observing a gannet working between the launch and the island, a deceptively sluggish bird and as graceful as the albatross. Abruptly, as though it had been shot, the gannet tips forward into a headlong dive with its wings still partly extended to give it command as, with the speed of a stone, it falls towards a shoal of surface fish. Only at the last instant do its wings fold tightly about itself as it enters the water with a splash.

Where that bird has dived there are small shoal fish, and where the shoal fish are there, too, probably are the bigger fish to chase and eat 'em. And where these bigger fish are there probably are the sharks and a swordfish or two. Taylor thumps the cabin decking and the bored steersman wakes up and alters the course of the launch toward the working gannets. The angler yawns and refrains from rubbing his sun-burned eyes.

All this day nothing happens to the bait-fish; but, as Sir Henry Wotton wrote of angling, it is "Idle time not idly spent".

Through his eyes every nerve of the angler's body receives a shock. Two yards behind the port teaser has appeared a fin, tapered in stream-lined beauty, cutting the water cleanly and giving no indication of the great body beneath it. The fin swerves outward from the darting cylinder of wood even whilst the angler draws in breath to shout:

"Swordie"!

With the agility of a cat on a wind-swayed branch, Taylor leaves his look-out position for'ard temporarily to take command at the wheel, giving orders for the teasers to be drawn inboard. The fin has dropped back and now is five or six yards behind the bait-fish, following it. The angler has donned body harness and clipped it to the rod reel. A gloved hand fingers the reel brake, ready to remove the slight brakeage preventing the bait-fish being taken out by the opposition of the water over which it is skimming.

During four or five seconds the fin keeps position behind the bait-fish. Then, with a gliding rush it is within a foot of the bait-fish. No one aboard the launch is conscious of time. What appears to be a minute is only a half-second. Over the bait-fish rises a brown pencil protruding from an elephantine mouth. The water swirls and the bait-fish vanishes. No more than that is seen of the giant fish.

In a split second the angler has removed these light brakeage from the reel, which begins its long screaming note as the line is taken away at yards per second, with his gloved left hand gently pressing on the revolving drum to prevent fatal over-winding at speed. Other than this he does nothing.

Swordfish caught off
Bermagui 1936. The
head, preserved, is
now in my lounge.

Fifty, a hundred, another fifty yards, two hundred yards of line is buried in the sea. As suddenly as it began, the reel ceases its scream. Still the angler does nothing. The launch has been stopped by Taylor, who gives the wheel over to his mate and comes to stand behind the angler. There is slackness in the line, which is quickly taken in. So far the rod has not been raised from its rest on the stern rail.

What is going on down there in the translucent depths?

The swordfish had taken the bait-fish in its gummy mouth. To have struck at that instant would have pulled the bait-fish clear. Like a mischievous dog, the swordfish had scampered away with the bait - at probably fifty miles an hour. Then it stopped, and is proceeding to scrunch the bait-fish and to swallow it.

Still the angler does nothing. Taylor and he are watching the section of cord between the rod tip and the water, and presently what they expect occurs to it. Its angle with the sea begins to be less acute, denoting that the fish is coming up.

The fish has felt the hook or the wire trace to which it is attached, and instantly its suspicions are aroused. Like a sea-sick ship's passenger rushing to the rail, the swordfish is coming to the surface to disgorge in air; for it cannot disgorge in the water as it is unable to swim backwards.

The angler's moment has arrived. It is now or never. The angler reels in line until he can feel the weight of the fish. Now he strikes by flashing upward the rod tip, up and over behind his head. As the rod tip flashes down so the line-slack gained is reeled in. Perhaps there is time to do all this again.

"There he goes! Look at him! O, what a beauty!"

Two hundred yards away the great fish is, apparently, dancing on its tail on the surface of the sea all a-glitter about his blue and green glittering form, his sword stabbing the cobalt sky, his head shaking like that of a reefing horse. Down he goes in a splather of foam leaping high to mark the spot. Up again he leaps to dance on his tail and to shake his head like an outlaw horse infuriated by restraint. It seems that he is in view for minutes: actually it is extremely difficult to photograph him with a snapshot camera.

Out of sight, he goes away. The reel screams as he takes with him another hundred yards of line. The angler, knowing the fish has failed to get rid of the hook, increases the reel brakeage and begins to fight. Half the line is out - quite enough. The rod, which he was unable to bend across a knee, is now become a bow. The fish stops and accepts the challenge to fight. Up the line to the rod traverses a succession of tremendously heavy tugs, the fish having taken the line round its tail or round its sword. Here is arrived the critical time when too much brakeage on the reel, producing over-tautness of the line, will snap the cord like cotton or snap the rod like a carrot.

With the cessation of the tugs the first round ends. Abruptly the line becomes ominously slack.

Now what! Has he got rid of the hook?

The angler rapidly reels in the slack. Ah! - the fish is still fast. Now the line is slanting away to the surface, far, farther.

"He's going to breach again!" Taylor shouts.

And there far away is the fish thrashing on the top of the diamond-flecked water, not now able to display himself so magnificently. Down he goes once more, again to bring anxiety to the angler by slackening the cord through swimming towards the launch.

"Have you lost him?" Taylor asks

"Dunno," replies the angler, reeling in line at his greatest speed. "He might have thrown it in that last jump. Ah - no! He's still there. I'll give it to him now."

The rod tip is raised against the strain and then, as it flashes downward so the slack gained is reeled in and held as the rod tip again is raised immediately above the angler's head. Thus ten, fifteen yards of cord are gained. Thus another twenty yards are got in on the reel drum. Then the strain becomes dangerous. The determined fish cannot be controlled. He takes out twenty yards of cord before again he is mastered.

Thirty-five minutes have elapsed since the bait-fish was taken. Still the angler is fighting to take in line, the stopped launch rolling and bucking, Taylor waiting for the orders from the angler, the mate waiting for orders from Taylor. With the aid of the body harness the rod is constantly raised to hold line and lowered to reel in the slack gained. The angler's left hand is "feeling" the strain on the line: his right controls the reel brake and the winding handle. On the hook is a fish weighing hundreds of pounds and the breaking strain of the line is far less than a hundred pounds.

Forty-five minutes have gone into this fight between this specimen of the greatest fighting fish of all and the man armed only with a frail rod and a line still more frail.

Now out of the water comes the glistening steel swivel connecting cord line with the wire trace. The fish is less than twenty yards away. Anyone standing on the cabin deck could see it below the surface. Come once more those terrific tugs and the fish gains thirty yards of line. He is not beaten yet by a long shot.

"He's too fresh to bring to the gaff!" shouts the angler.

"Too right!" agrees Taylor. "Play him a bit more. If he jumps here, we'll all get wet. Look out! He's going to breach!"

And there, a mere fifty yards away, there appears the great head and sword. The fish raises itself half way up above the surface. It shakes its head, sinks, rises again to shake its head and to beat its sword upon the water.

It is the end of a great fight put up by a noble fighter. There is no more "sting" in this fish and sorrowfully it is drawn to the gaff, roped and hauled on board.

A perfect day having a perfect ending, one worth living for years to experience. The sun is sinking and the launch is headed for Bermagui, away up at the mast top the blue flag of triumph flying.

THESE HOISTED THE FLAG IN 1937-38

NAME	ADDRESS	FISH	WEIGHT	DATE	LAUNCH
E. & W. Bullen	Sydney	Mako	400 lbs.	19th Dec.	Vida
Denis Moore	Melbourne	S. Marlin	237 ,,	20th Dec.	Merlin
Denis Moore	Melbourne	B. Marlin	280 ,,	21st Dec.	Merlin
P. Ebeling	Sydney	S. Marlin	260 ,,	27th Dec.	Gladious
W. Bullen	Sydney	Mako	180 ,,	1st Jan.	Vida
Bruce Jonas	Sydney	Hammerhead	269 ,,	5th Jan.	Gladious
A. W. Curtis	Sydney	S. Marlin	202 ,,	11th Jan.	Vida
L. S. Brookes	Sydney	B. Marlin	232 ,,	15th Jan.	Merlin
A. W. Curtis	Sydney	S. Marlin	222 ,,	19th Jan.	Vida
J. W. Weatherill	Sydney	B. Marlin	164 ,,	20th Jan.	Vida
Les. Stewart	Melbourne	Mako	277 ,,	24th Jan.	Excel
L. Stewart	Melbourne	Hammerhead	259 ,,	24th Jan.	Excel

Australian Record Black Marlin, 672 lbs., caught by
Mr. J. R. Porter, of Melbourne, on 22nd January, 1937.

43

Upfield with a 274 lb Marlin caught on 10 February 1938.

NAME	ADDRESS	FISH	WEIGHT	DATE	LAUNCH
C. W. Firth	Sydney	B. Marlin	197 lbs.	25th Jan.	Edith
C. W. Firth	Sydney	S. Marlin	210 ,,	28th Jan.	Edith
A. W. Taylor	Narrandera	Hammerhead	138 ,,	28th Jan.	Gladious
Alan Blacka	Cobargo	B. Marlin	200 ,,	29th Jan.	Gladious
W. Winter	Melbourne	S. Marlin	238 ,,	30th Jan.	Merlin
A. Upfield	Mt. Dandenong	B. Marlin	260 ,,	30th Jan.	Gladious
C. W. Firth	Sydney	S. Marlin	208 ,,	30th Jan.	Edith
A. Upfield	Mt. Dandenong	B. Marlin	260 ,,	2nd Feb.	Gladious
J. Carolin	Melbourne	Hammerhead	260 ,,	5th Feb.	Excel
R. Michaelis	Melbourne	B. Marlin	250 ,,	6th Feb.	Excel
Dr. D. Stevens	Melbourne	Hammerhead	416 ,,	8th Feb.	Excel
G. L. Lansell	Melbourne	B. Marlin	214 ,,	9th Feb.	Excel
A. Upfield	Mt. Dandenong	B. Marlin	274 ,,	10th Feb.	Gladious
O. Woodhouse	Cooma	B. Marlin	226 ,,	10th Feb.	Coo-ee
Chas. Stewart	Sydney	B. Marlin	182 ,,	11th Feb.	Vida
Chas. Stewart	Sydney	S. Marlin	180 ,,	11th Feb.	Vida
S. R. Syme	Melbourne	B. Marlin	204 ,,	11th Feb.	Merlin
J. T. Drake	Mansfield	B. Marlin	277 ,,	12th Feb.	Excel
Dr. Ray Allen	Sydney	S. Marlin	250 ,,	13th Feb.	Vida
J. W. Bucknell	Yass	S. Marlin	220 ,,	14th Feb.	Edith
Chas. Stewart	Sydney	S. Marlin	314 ,,	16th Feb.	Vida
Dr. Ray Allen	Sydney	S. Marlin	212 ,,	16th Feb.	Vida
Pat. Osborne	Harden	B. Marlin	246 ,,	16th Feb.	Myoni
A. Towart	Holbrook	B. Marlin	238 ,,	17th Feb.	Gladious
N. Mc. Kinnell	Melbourne	B. Marlin	286 ,,	18th Feb.	Merlin
Alan Bowler	Holbrook	S. Marlin	278 ,,	24th Feb.	Gladious
A. F. Saunders	Warren	Whaler Shark	238 ,,	24th Feb.	Snowy
C. W. Firth	Sydney	S. Marlin	160 ,,	26th Feb.	Edith
Chas. Stewart	Sydney	B. Marlin	282 ,,	27th Feb.	Vida
W. F. Laidlaw	Melbourne	Hammerhead	460 ,,	27th Feb.	Excel
G. W. Brown	Melbourne	Hammerhead	348 ,,	27th Feb.	Gladious
W. K. Fagan	Mandurama	S. Marlin	206 ,,	1st March	Ivy
Les. Winkworth	Sydney	Tiger Shark	572 ,,	2nd March	Gladious
W. Hechle	Albury	S. Marlin	260 ,,	4th March	Lily G.
W. Hechle	Albury	S. Marlin	172 ,,	4th March	Lily G.
O. Hart	Melbourne	Mako	200 ,,	3rd March	Coo-ee
P. Ebeling	Sydney	Hammerhead	320 ,,	4th March	Myoni
P. Ebeling	Sydney	S. Marlin	174 ,,	7th March	Myoni
W. Gray	Lockhart	B. Marlin	202 ,,	7th March	Merlin
B. Hickling	Melbourne	S. Marlin	287 ,,	7th March	Gladious
Chas. Smith	Albury	Whaler Shark	370 ,,	8th March	Lily G.
C. W. Firth	Sydney	S. Marlin	220 ,,	9th March	Edith
W. F. Laidlaw	Melbourne	B. Marlin	162 ,,	9th March	Excel
C. Hughes	Sydney	Hammerhead	270 ,,	13th March	Edith
S. Jackson	Melbourne	Hammerhead	414 ,,	17th March	Vida
R. L. Cox	Melbourne	Hammerhead	184 ,,	18th March	Vida
L. E. Burt	Sydney	S. Marlin	260 ,,	20th March	Edith
R. Cox	Melbourne	S. Marlin	276 ,,	20th March	Vida
Alan Blacka	Cobargo	Hammerhead	302 ,,	20th March	Gladious
C. W. Firth	Sydney	Hammerhead	290 ,,	21st March	Excel
G. Mac. Nathan	Trangie	S. Marlin	260 ,,	22nd March	Dorothea
L. E. Burt	Sydney	Hammerhead	222 ,,	25th March	Edith
J. L. Myers	Manila	S. Marlin	280 ,,	29th March	Vida
C. W. Firth	Sydney	Kingfish	88 ,,	14th April	Edith
			(Aust. Record 12 thread line)		
P. Ebeling	Sydney	Hammerhead	300 ,,	16th April	Gladious
Percy Ebeling	Sydney	White Shark	488 ,,	18th April	Gladious
John Bell	Melbourne	Hammerhead	201 ,,	18th April	Excel
T. A. Bell	Melbourne	Tiger Shark	1151. ,,	20th April	Excel
			(World's Record)		
R. J. Fagan	Mandurama	S. Marlin	220 ,,	22nd April	Ivy

5.

BIG GAME FISHING IN AUSTRALIA

THE sea snarls: "No you won't!" And the river hisses: "Yes, I will!" For centuries the Pacific Ocean has been thus arguing with the Bermaguee River, situated some 250 miles south of Sydney and so named by the Aborigines for a meeting place of the waters. The struggle is ceaseless, the sea trying to block the river with sand, and the river maintaining a narrow channel across the sand-bar deep enough for the passage of fifty-foot launches.

During the winter months the prevailing current-set is from the cold South. Then, a day in September, will appear on the calm surface of a bay a dark patch which will remain a little while, disappear and reappear elsewhere. The patch is caused by a shoal of sprats, the heralds of the army of surface fish coming from the waters of the Barrier Reef.

The greatest of all fish food is the Plankton, a tiny shrimp-like creature, pale in colour and swimming jerkily as it keeps within the bounds of the warm current. Strangely enough, a warm current isn't always on, or close to the surface, although never deep down. On a blazing hot day the temperature of the water 20 feet below is often higher than that nearest the sun, and these currents are themselves patches so that, even in summer there are vast water-patches where there is no plankton… and no shoal fish.

The plankton must live on something smaller than itself, but will go on farther down the scale. The sprats live on the plankton, so do the barracoota, tuna and many of the whales. The sharks live on the larger fish, as do the swordfish. Thus, following a circle, where the plankton is there, too, will be the sharks and the swordfish.

Twenty-five years ago little if anything was known about the marlin in these waters so far south of the tropics. When the local fisherman saw a slim, more rounded than triangular dorsal fin slicing through the water at great speed they attributed it to yet another shark. It did not arrive with the plankton, and it disappeared well before the plankton went back north. Then someone saw a strange fish leap, saw its slim head and long 'sword' and persuaded two anglers to test the sea. They caught eleven marlin in one day, a number that has never been surpassed.

The catch comprised two types: the striped marlin, long, slim and very fast, and the black marlin, chunky, powerful, a dour fighter. Then Zane Grey came to Bermagui, the township's spelling, and big game fishing in Australia was established.

Shall we go out big game fishing? To succeed you must be rigidly self-controlled, possessed of the virtue of patience, and have a workable imagination. Otherwise you are going to break or lose valuable equipment.

The launch and the crew of two are ready for sea at eight o'clock. The barometer is high but the weathermen have forecast a southerly change accompanied by wind. In the low stern is the angler's chair. Pivoted to turn where desired, and to the edge of the chair is bolted the butt of the great rod carrying a heavy steel reel which may be braked to control the 900 yards of line having a snapping strain of 90 lbs. When seated in the chair, the rod is between the angler's knees, and the reel is clipped to the angler's body harness. Thus, he cannot be rolled overboard.

There is no fishing comparable to this.

With bait-fish to hand, the side poles are lowered, and from these are trailed imitation fish called teasers to ride the water either side of the craft and twenty feet astern. A bonito or kingfish is tied to the angler's hook at the extremity of twelve to sixteen feet of wire trace which in turn is knotted to the cord line. With the bait-fish riding thirty feet behind the teasers, maintained there by the breaking action of the angler's reel, there are three small fish forever trying to catch up with the launch.

Now all is ready for the big fish.

There is an unwritten law, unfortunately not always observed, intended to favor the game fish and demanding of the angler extreme patience and wisdom. Zane Grey never used more than one hook buried in his bait-fish, and far more often than not he was satisfied with bringing in one marlin to the gaff per day. To use more than one hook is not unlike caging a lion before you shoot it.

The wind is coming from the north-east, and the sea is a little choppy as the wind is against the low ground swell coming up from the south. The air is free of spin-drift and land-smoke. The water is remarkably clear and like liquid turquoise.

To port, left-side, the coast curves away in a great bay behind which is Dromedary Mountain, a 2000-footer. Eight miles up the coast is Montague Island, with its lighthouse. On its rocks bask the seals, and amid the dunes burrow the penguins. To starboard is the Pacific Ocean, or that part of it between Australia and New Zealand called the Tasman Sea.

A gannet flies by before abruptly nose-diving, to fold its wings tight at the instant it meets the water like a dropped stone. An excellent sign. You can count six before it re-appears, with a sprat in its beak. An albatross 'floats' with unsurpassed grace over the launch, its long black eyes watchful, its snowy breast and under-wings taking the blue dye of the sea. Were those birds not working today, we may as well go home. One launchman steers, the other keeps a look-out ahead. The angler watches his bait-fish and the teasers, waiting with hope strong in him.

It is anticipation of battle that is the real thrill of this sport, for an angler can watch his bait-fish all day, for several days, and see nothing else. Soon he feels he is the fourth fish frantically trying to keep up with the launch and the safety of its shadow, ever spurred by the threat of unseen monsters.

Suddenly the course is altered. The launch is steered for a patch of dark water not agitated by the wind or cross-currents.

The black patch on the blue and white overlay betrays the presence of shoal fish under which might be a shark. Distance decreasing, the disturbed area usually spreads to cover an acre, and then anything up to a square mile. Outside the area the waves behave normally: within, the waves are flattened and short ridges run everywhere. Fish, by the ton! Enough fish in this one shoal to sink a 10,000 ton ship. Tuna! Yellow-fin! You can see them beyond the face of the swells, fish without number, but in this shoal all of the same size, all close to fourteen pounds. There are shoals containing 20-pounders only. No wonder man can watch tuna until they drop with sheer exhaustion.

Close to the launch, ignoring it, appears a long blue-grey torpedo prowed by an iron-hard brown 'sword'. It leaps forward like a leased hound straining after a hare. Before it the water is churned white by frantic fish trying to escape that spear smashing down upon them, shattering some, wounding to death many others. The marlin couldn't miss, and down he goes to swim back to feed on the pieces before the fish blood brings a shark or two.

As suddenly as the marlin disappeared, so do the yellow-fin, and the sea is again empty, or appears so. The launch is steered in circles, the hope being to attract the marlin with the teasers and bait-fish. Nothing appears to break the wavelets. Until… Three yards behind the bait-fish a fin rises, a large triangular fin having a dull white spot in its centre. A shark. A Mako. One second the empty sea, that ugly sinister fin tracking the bait-fish like an aborigine.

"Fish-oh!" shouts the angler.

Pity the bait-fish! Looking so desperately alive! Run! Run! RUN!

The great fin weaves through the water, draws close. Then it angles side-wise, and up beside the bait-fish appears a grey-brown snout, blunt, gashed by a widening cavern all water-washed and gleaming with teeth. Amid the swirl, the bait-fish vanishes, and the snout sinks down into the sea.

Everything seems to happen at once. The reel screams as the line is torn from it at many feet per second. The launch is stopped. A man is assisting the angler into his body harness of leather and straps, and a thong from the harness is clipped to the rod reel.

The angler needs to be patient with the monster. He lifts the rod up and gently applies the reel brake. Feeling the brakeage on the line, he flashes upward the rod tip so that what has gone into the shark's maw will be buried there. He can feel the fish, and lowering the rod, tightens again on the line and flashes upward the rod tip.

The shark is hooked. Away he goes at speed, and downward, and nothing the angler can do now will stop him because he weighs probably 300 pounds and more, and the breaking strain on the line, is only 90 lbs. Abruptly the reel ceases to scream. The angler waits.

What is going on a hundred feet down and three hundred feet from the launch? The shark is wondering what's wrong with that morsel of fish that seems to be trying to get away. The mako is beginning to think. The angler, the fingers of his left hand caressing the line, can almost 'feel' its thinking. He believes he can actually feel the Beast sawing at the steel trace.

It's coming up. It's now angry. As it comes up it rolls, feeling the line drag, testing the trace, becoming every second more infuriated with this thing that is fighting him.

He is pounding the surface to suds, a mass of dull-grey amid the snowy-white. The angler is constantly raising the rod tip, lowering it to wind in line. The shark is shaking his head like a water dog, and if the angler isn't careful one of those head tugs will surely snap the line, and perhaps even snap the rod. "Careful, sir," whispers the launchman, even more anxious than his angler. Everything depends on the angler's use of the brake, and his ability to think ahead of the shark.

Then like most of us, when the shark loses his temper he ceases to think, and when he does, he's done for, providing the angler doesn't cease thinking. If the shark continued to think it could have wound the line around his powerful tail, jerked twice and snapped the line as if it were cotton. That is if he caught the angler off guard. But he isn't thinking any more. He is rushing off in that direction, then off in another, and every time he seems to be free he is braked hard, and as the minutes pass he tires though his rage remains as terrible.

Presently the angler brings the mako within yards of the launch which it can see as it thrashes about on the surface; and now rage is rivalled by hatred and it rushes towards the launch, pauses when a few yards from it like a horse about to jump, and then literally springs over the water to get at the angler.

It was expected. The leap falls short. The shark is spent, but by no means harmless. The angler must play it still for a few minutes before bringing it to the gaff, and all the 350 pounds of it is dragged on board to be taken back to the jetty and officially weighed.

Mako, grey nurse, white whaler, hammerhead, all these are smaller than the monsters never seen near the surface save on very rare occasions. There was the unidentified shark estimated by experienced launchmen at seventy feet in length, which rose beside the craft and kept even pace with it, and they swear that now and then it winked its awful eyes at them. They could have speared it, but feared it might smash in the timbers with its tail. It behaved similarly with other launches.

There is no mistaking the dorsal fin of a marlin. It doesn't waggle like that of a shark. It cuts through the water, straight and clean, and is reputed to travel normally at sixty miles an hour. It is like a rapier compared with a bludgeon, a racehorse with a lumbering turtle. It thinks and fights and never loses its temper. You cannot loathe it like a shark.

This one circled the launch, and the men waited. No-one shouted fish-oh. Then the fin disappeared, to come up behind the bait-fish, to trail its scent for a quarter-mile as though to tease the angler into a fit. The harness was about the angler and hooked to the rod reel when the elephantine mouth gracefully rose over the bait-fish and the reel began its screaming.

The line ran away like cotton on a reel to be wound upon a bobbin. The angler and the launchman watch the cord on the reel dwindle and dwindle, the angler's right hand gently braking, until half of the 900 yards is buried in the sea when the run stops.

The fish is down deep. It is turning the bait-fish over and over in its teeth-less jaws, crunching it preparatory to swallowing it head first. A move by the angler would snatch the bait-fish away. He can but wait. He watches he angle of the line with the plane of the sea, then sees by the alteration of the angle that the fish is coming up.

The marlin has felt the hook, and there is only one possible way of getting rid of it. As the fish must always move forward, the only way to be rid of the hook is to disgorge it in the air.

As it comes up the angler must strike... flashing upward the rod tip, lowering it and gaining line, braking and raising again, and so on and on.

There he is. Up from the glittering sea springs the loveliest creature in all the oceans. It appears to dance upon its tail, the tail resting on purest snow, the utterly perfect body enshrined by a mist of rainbow colours. It shakes its long head, and the 'sword' thrusts at the cobalt sky in royal defiance.

How long does it dance? Three seconds, sometimes four. Time doesn't matter. Down he goes, off and away deep down, to come up for a second dance which is nothing like the first.

Following the last dance, the fish tears away, and the line leaps after it into the deep. There is only 900 yards all told so he must be stopped before he takes 850 of those yards. The brake goes on a little harder, and beside the brakeage there is all the line buried in the sea to brake the fish, too. Abruptly, it stops to think.

Now, you angler, watch out!

The fish tries to wind the line round himself, and if he succeeds, the drag will be off his mouth. The angler must fight him without pause. The unwritten law is being observed, and the only hook could be torn from the mouth once the fish gained the purchase with his tail. No go! Try another. He races back toward the boat, and now the angler must wind in line and is unable to wind fast enough. Water pours off the reel, sweat pours off the angler. The steersman must keep the stern of the launch to the fish, and the angler's assistant can only prance with anxiety. Then the fish sheers away. There is fatal slack of the line not brought to the reel. The fish is rolling slowly, trying to get his 'sword' around the cord, trying to gain a purchase and snap it when the angler does gain the slack.

In comes the slack. The line becomes taut... just for a fraction of a second before the brake is right off. The fish wangs its 'sword', but as there is no brakeage on the line, there is no resistance. Minutes pass while the fish tries trick after trick and controlled only by a thread which never yields and yet never tautly resists.

Slowly the fish tires, becomes exhausted by being partially immobilised in the element through which it must pass at speed. He will fight to the last, and a 300-pounder will wear out an angler after a fight of forty-five minutes.

Now he is lying beside the shark, a thing of iridescent beauty, of superb stream-lined grace against the filthy tiger of the deep.

The marlin didn't win. This angler, and his boatmen, have looked at a severed line and cheered a marlin that did.

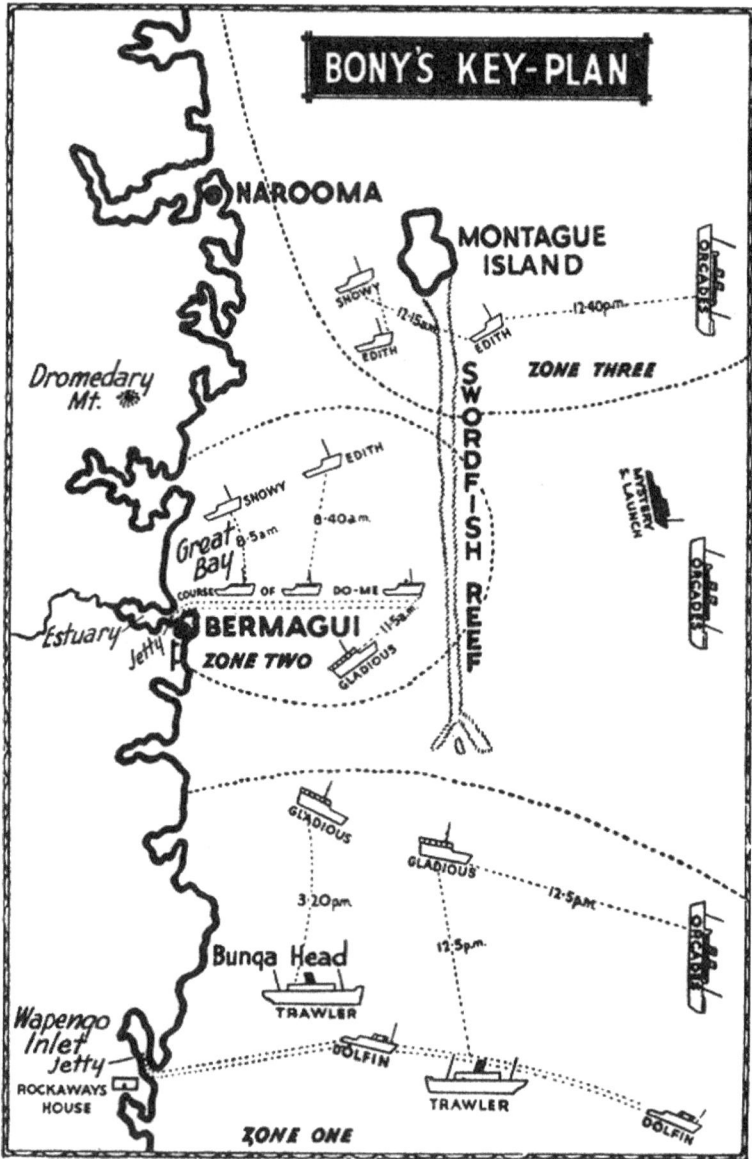

Bony's key-plan to *The Mystery of Swordfish Reef*, published in 1939.

6.

A CLUE AMONG FISH

Before the construction of the Prince's Highway, Bermagui was an isolated hamlet aroused only at Christmas and at Easter by the small influx of visitors from inland farms and the market town of Cobargo. Even after the opening of the Highway it suffered to some extent through the disadvantage of being seven miles from it at Tilba Tilba. It was His Majesty the Swordfish that "made" Bermagui.

The discovery of swordfish in the waters off the southern coast of New South Wales was due to chance, for their swift-moving dorsal fins when seen by the fishermen were thought to be a species of shark. A fisherman when out for salmon, using a hand line with a feathered hook attached, one afternoon was bringing to his boat a fine fighting salmon which was followed by a huge fish. The big fish came to the surface close to the boat—to reveal not only its dorsal fin but its "sword".

For some time this was thought to be only a fisherman's yarn, until Mr Roy Smith determined to test the story, and on 2nd February, 1933, proved its authenticity by capturing with rod and reel a black marlin weighing 262 pounds. Still, doubt remained general that swordfish regularly visited the coast of southern New South Wales, although the fishermen declared that the swift-moving fins had been seen every summer. When Mr Roy Machaelis and Mr W. G. Wallis between them captured nine swordfish in the one day, deep sea anglers the world over began to take notice. The subsequent visit of Mr Zane Grey resulted in Bermagui becoming famous as a centre of big game angling.

When Angler Ericson and his launchmen on the *Do-me* vanished, Bermagui suffered a slight setback, for it naturally followed that when an unexplained catastrophe overwhelmed a small launch the other launches were considered to be too frail for the open sea, or too likely to be the victims of whales or mermen, or too liable to strike an uncharted reef. Proof of this came quickly in the form of cancelled bookings of the launches and hotel accommodation.

The search for the *Do-me* achieved nothing but the reclamation of one thermos-flask from the sea.

Detective-Sergeant Allen's reputation was high, but he was unfortunately a poor sailor. Jack Wilton and Joe took him out to show him the position of the Gladious when Remmings last sighted the *Do-me,* and the position of the *Do-me* when she was last sighted, but poor Allen became frightfully sea-sick and unable to maintain any interest. Thereafter he confined his investigating to the land.

One man in Bermagui came to wonder just who and what Mr Ericson had been—and was, if still alive. The secretary of the club followed the intensive and extensive search with both hope for its success and gratification that officialdom was trying so hard, incidentally, to remove the stigma the mystery put upon Bermagui.

A second plane was sent down from Sydney to assist the first in its thorough examination of the sea and the coast. Allen recommended the employment of the Marlin, and her crew, to continue making a search for flotsam, and for a little more than a fortnight Wilton and his mate enjoyed government pay. On shore, Sergeant Allen organised two search-parties to explore the base of cliffs and those parts of the coast barred to launches, these men primarily concentrating on the discovery of small items of wreckage not likely to be observed by the air pilots. At the end of three weeks the only clue to the fate of the *Do-me* was the thermos-flask retrieved from the sea by Wilton.

Even the flask was not a clue that proved anything. That it belonged to the licensee of the Bermagui Hotel, and that it had been filled with tea and put into Ericson's lunch basket, was, of course, established; but, there was no proof how it came to be floating in the sea; whether it had been washed off the *Do-me* when she sank, or had been lost overboard. General opinion favoured the first theory; for, as Joe Peace maintained, had the angler or one of his launchmen accidentally knocked the flask overboard it would have been retrieved. It appeared unlikely that an article such as a thermos-flask would fall overboard unobserved. The angler would take it from the basket, and pour tea from it, whilst he was in his rightful place—the cockpit.

Joe's claim to the wide knowledge of the local sea currents, and his ability to follow them, even to "back-track" them, was given little credence by Sergeant Allen, or by Detective-Sergeant Light, who came down to assist him. The small army of reporters were even greater doubters. For a while Bermagui accommodation was taxed to its utmost, and the official search was maintained for three weeks.

No wonder that Mr Blade began to think that the missing angler was a world figure incognito. After Light went back to Sydney in one of the planes, and the search parties were disbanded, Wilton and Joe continued to search for evidence of the fate of the *Do-me*, and Constable Telfer confided in Blade when telling him that Sergeant Allen had received instructions to remain on the "job" until recalled.

October passed out in calm and warm weather. But November quickly produced a nor'-easterly which raged for days and kept the launches idle and the few anglers in the hotel bar.

After that one terrible night and day of vigil Mrs Spinks became almost normal. Almost but not quite, for her mind appeared to have become permanently deranged on one matter. She refused to believe that the *Do-me* was lost and that her son was dead. She took advantage of every opportunity to escape from the watchful care of her daughter and would hurry to the headland to search the ocean for sight of her son's launch coming home. Often she called in on Mr Blade to request him to send to a passing ship a wireless message asking the captain to tell her son to return at once as his underclothes were due to be changed.

The neighbours and others felt pity and little wonder because in her belief that the *Do-me* had not gone down Mrs Spinks was firmly supported by Marion, whose mind had not been affected by the tragedy. The only change to be observed in Marion was the absence of her flashing laughter. She would shake her head when people proffered sympathy and say:

"Bill's not dead. I'd know it if he was dead."

The sixth day of November was indelibly printed on Blade's mind by visits he received in the afternoon from Jack Wilton and, later, a visiting angler, a Mr George Emery. Wilton did not expend time in preliminaries.

"I've come to see you about Marion and Mrs Spinks," he said, his brown eyes a little troubled but his mouth determined. "They're in a bad way—about money. As you know, old man Spinks was a boozer and left the family well in debt when he died. It was only then that Bill got a square deal from life and began to pull things together. The building of the *Do-me* put him in debt again, but he had cleared this off just before the *Do-me* vanished.

"Other times Marion would have got a job somewhere, but now she has to look after her mother more than ever she did after the old man pegged out. I'm in love with Marion. Been that way since we were kids at school. And I wanted her to marry me—want her to marry me now—but she couldn't make up her mind about it. And now she's not trying. I want you to do me a favour. Will you?"

"Of course, Jack."

"Well, I've been thinking of getting up a subscription to help them two, but it wouldn't do for me to run it, Marion being a bit proud and independent. I've got here a hundred quid. Just took it out of the bank. You could say you had received it from a rich sympathizer in Sydney or somewhere."

Placing the money in a compact bundle on the table, he put down beside it a smaller sheaf of notes, saying:

"This is from my partner, Joe Peace. There's twenty-seven quid in it. That makes a hundred and twenty-seven. If you could raise another twenty-three to make the total a hundred and fifty, it could be suggested to Marion that she take over Nott's shop. Mrs Nott wants to go to Melbourne to live, and she's willing to sell for a hundred and fifty and the balance at interest."

Blade's gaze moved from the eager face to his typewriter. He did not look up when he asked:

"Would Miss Spinks go into that business, do you think?"

"I think so—so long as I had nothing to do with it. We were talking about it last night. She says she thinks her mother wouldn't be so restless if she had to prepare the teas and suppers and make the meat-pies."

"Very well, Jack. I'll raise the balance."

"Thanks, Mr Blade. I thought you'd help. You'll keep me and Joe out of it?"

"Yes, as you wish it."

Blade saw that his visitor waited, but hesitated, to suggest something further.

"You can depend on me to do everything I can to help Miss Spinks and her mother," he said encouragingly.

"Good! And—and would you keep an eye on the books and things? You see, Marion and me aren't good at that part of it."

"I shall be glad to, Jack."

Wilton rose to his feet, his face swept clean of trouble.

"Things is going to be droughty with us this summer," he said, thoughtfully. "Not with the ordinary people, but with us launch-men. Two of my bookings for the swordies have been cancelled and the others have had bookings cancelled too. Me and Joe will have to take to the beach-netting for salmon for the factory. It's a blasted shame we can't sell tunny. There's millions of 'em about now. All from six- to fifteen-pounders."

Blade smiled.

"I don't think we need worry much, Jack. The *Do-me* affair will blow over by Christmas now that the newspapers have shut down on it."

Wilton had not been gone ten minutes when Mr Emery entered. He was portly, important, and now burned scarlet by the wind and sun and sea-spray. He advanced with hand outstretched.

"I'm leaving for Sydney, Blade. Business calls and all that. Blast business! Should have gone yesterday, you know, but this fishing gets into a man's very bones."

"Well, I hope you will come again soon."

Mr Emery beamed, but was explosive.

"Come again! Hang it, Blade! I couldn't keep away if every launch in Bermagui disappeared. I'm coming down for the swordies early in January. It's a bit rough on those women, anyway. Saw them last evening on the headland when we were coming in. The daughter was trying to persuade the mother to go home with her, or it looked like it."

It was then that Blade had inspiration. He first bound Mr Emery to confidence and then related what had transpired between Wilton and himself. Mr Emery said, less explosively:

"Give me a pen."

He wrote his cheque hurriedly, and rose to his feet, saying:

"Give them two fellers back their savings. If I can't still make three hundred pounds before breakfast I'm losing my punch. So long, and if you can spare a minute any time drop me a letter saying how the fish are going. I'm only living for the swordies in January."

He shook hands, beamed and departed, leaving Blade a little breathless and staring down at the cheque he had drawn in Marion's favour for three hundred pounds. The figures were written with extreme care, but the signature was familiar to the secretary, although he was unable to read it. Blade was astonished but not amazed, for swordfishing is a rich man's sport, and rich men sometimes are philanthropic.

Marion Spinks and her mother were in possession of the refreshment shop and small store by the middle of November. The girl's hopes were justified; so long as Mrs. Spinks could be kept busy she appeared not to worry about her son's clean underclothes. There were occasions, however, especially towards evening, when Mrs Spinks would slip away to the headland, and then Marion had to run to Mrs Wilton and ask her to "mind" the shop whilst she went after her mother.

Shortly before four o'clock on the afternoon of the 20th, there appeared rounding the headland to reach the steamer wharf a rusty and disreputable ship of some two thousand tons. The only respectable portion of her was her bridge, white-painted and almost entirely glassed in. On either side of her blunt bow was the cipher *A.S.3.*

It so happened that, when the *A.S.3* hove into sight of those about the only street of Bermagui, Edward Blade was talking with Detective-Sergeant Allen and Mr Parkins, the garage proprietor, outside the club secretary's office.

"Hullo! What does she want in here?" demanded Mr Parkins, a keen-eyed man of fifty. "I haven't seen one of those trawlers here for a long time."

"So that's a trawler, it is?" mildly inquired Sergeant Allen, the very sight of this ship arousing memory of his excessive sea-sickness.

"Yes," Blade answered him. "It might be that one of her crew has met with an accident. There must be something serious, for her captain to call here. Let's go along and find out."

The three men walked along the street, past the hotel, deserted at this time of day and of the week, and so reached the edge of the wharf as two men in a small boat were returning from having taken a rope hawser to the mooring buoy. The captain was giving megaphone orders to his crew.

The ship was being gently "edged" to the wharf front with the aid of propeller and winch. The actions of the men hinted that the ship's stay at Bermagui was not to be overlong. Immediately aft of the bridge was the wireless cabin, and in the doorway of this was standing the operator, a young man who appeared either delicate in health or still suffering from sea-sickness. The captain having done with his megaphone, Blade shouted:

"Anything wrong, Captain?"

"Nothing much," came the shouted answer. "I'm wanting the constable. Suppose he's about?"

"Well, no, he's out of town this afternoon. Had a mutiny?"

The crew were passing a gangway from ship to wharf. The captain left his bridge, gained the deck, and passed along the gangway to Blade and his companions.

"When will the constable be back?" demanded the trawler captain. "Can't stay here in port all day."

"Not until this evening, Captain. But if you have trouble of any kind, here is Detective-Sergeant Allen, who will take charge of it."

"Oh, good day, Sergeant. Please follow me."

The captain recrossed the gangway, followed by Allen with Blade and Parkins. The small procession made its way across the littered deck to the bridge entrance where it was calmly surveyed by the first mate. Blade had noticed whilst they were on the main deck how the crew stared at them, and as he mounted to the bridge he noticed the fixed expression on the face of the wireless operator and received a shock from the look of stark horror in the young man's eyes. The captain halted beside the ship's wheel at the foot of which a piece of old tarpaulin lay heaped as though it covered a small object. Grimly the captain said:

"At two-thirty this afternoon, I gave the order for the trawl to be brought inboard. The trawl had been down on the sea bottom for one hour thirty minutes, when the course of the ship had been roughly parallel with Swordfish Reef and half a mile inshore of it. Among the fish and other stuff in the trawl was this—"

He bent down swiftly and snatched up the piece of tarpaulin.

Mr Parkins cried loudly:

"Good lord!"

Blade whistled, and Sergeant Allen hissed between his teeth.

Grinning up at them from the bridge flooring was a human head.

`Its aspect was much more horrific than those polished relics to be found in museums. Although the flesh had been removed by the crayfish and the crabs and small fish the scalp still covered the cranium, and to the scalp was still attached dark-grey hair.

Blade knew that he felt much like the wireless operator was still feeling. He regarded Allen as a strong man when the detective bent down the closer to examine the fearful object. Mr Parkins did not move. The captain's voice appeared to reach him from great distance.

"This head has been in the water less than months and longer than days," the captain was remarking. "It might belong to one of those poor fellows on the launch *Do-me*."

"There was only the head—no body?" asked Allen.

"No, Sergeant, there was no body … only that. I haven't yet figured it out how it came to get into the trawl, the lower edge of the trawl being slightly above the sea bottom, if you know what I mean. By rights the trawl ought to have passed over it. Just a fluke, I suppose. Funny how murder will out, isn't it?"

"Funny!" gasped Mr Parkins, and the captain glared at him.

"Murder!" Allen said softly.

The captain again stooped, and this time when he straightened he held the relic between his hands. He held it high; held it level with the eyes of the three men. Just behind the right temple they saw a neat round hole. The captain reversed the head, and then they saw much farther back from the left temple another hole, larger and less neat.

"Bullet-holes," said Sergeant Allen.

"Bullet-holes," echoed Blade.

"That's what I think," agreed the captain. "The poor feller who once had this head on his walking body wasn't drowned. He was shot, murdered."

"And he was on board the *Do-me*," Mr Parkins added. "Look at the hair! It must be Mr Ericson's head."

Chapter 4 from Upfield's *The Mystery of Swordfish Reef* (1939)

7.

WISP OF WOOL AND DISK OF SILVER

IT was Sunday. The heat drove the blowflies to roost under the low staging that supported the iron tank outside the kitchen door. The small flies, apparently created solely for the purpose of drowning themselves in the eyes of man and beast, were not noticed by the man lying on the rough bunk set up under the verandah roof. He was reading a mystery story.

The house was of board, and iron-roofed. Nearby were other buildings: a blacksmith's shop, a truck shed, and a junk house. Beyond them a windmill raised water to a reservoir tank on high stilts, which in turn fed a long line of troughing. This was the outstation at the back of Reefer's Find.

Reefer's Find was a cattle ranch. It was not a large station for Australia – a mere half-million acres within its boundary fence. The outstation was forty-odd miles from the main homestead, and that isn't far in Australia.

Only one rider lived at the outstation – Harry Larkin, who was, this hot Sunday afternoon, reading a mystery story. He had been quartered there for more than a year, and every night at seven o'clock, the boss at the homestead telephoned to give orders for the following day and to be sure he was still alive and kicking. Usually, Larkin spoke to a man face to face about twice a month.

Larkin might have talked to a man more often had he wished. His nearest neighbor lived nine miles away in a small stockman's hut on the next property, and once they had often met at the boundary by prearrangement. But then Larkin's neighbour, whose name was William Reynolds, was a difficult man, according to Larkin, and the meetings stopped.

On all sides of this small homestead the land stretched flat to the horizon. Had it not been for the scanty, narrow-leafed mulga and the sick-looking sandalwood trees, plus the mirage which turned a salt bush into a Jack's beanstalk and a tree into a telegraph pole stuck on a bald man's head, the horizon would have been as distant as that of the ocean.

A man came stalking through the mirage, the blanket roll on his back making him look like a ship standing on its bowsprit. The lethargic dogs were not aware of the visitor until he was about ten yards from the verandah. So engrossed was Larkin that even the barking of his dogs failed to distract his attention, and the stranger actually reached the edge of the verandah floor and spoke before Larkin was aware of him.

"He, he! Good day, mate! Flamin' hot today, ain't it?"

Larkin swung his legs off the bunk and sat up. What he saw was not usual in this part of Australia – a sundowner, a bush waif who tramps from north to south or from east to west, never working, cadging rations from the far-flung homesteads and having the ability of the camel to do without water, or find it. Sometimes Old Man Sun tricked one of them, and then the vast bushland took him and never gave up the cloth-tattered skeleton.

"Good day," Larkin said, to add with ludicrous inanity, "Travelling?"

"Yes, mate. Makin' down south." The derelict slipped the swag off his shoulder and sat on it. "What place is this?"

Larkin told him. "Mind me camping here tonight, mate? Wouldn't be in the way. Wouldn't be here in the mornin', either."

"You can camp over in the shed," Larkin said. "And if you pinch anything, I'll track you and belt the guts out of you."

A vacuous grin spread over the dust-grimed, bewhiskered face.

"Me, mate? I wouldn't pinch nothin'. Could do with a pinch of tea, and a bit of flour. He, he! Pinch – I mean a fistful of tea and sugar, mate."

Five minutes of this bird would send a man crazy. Larkin entered the kitchen, found an empty tin, and poured into it an equal quantity of tea and sugar. He scooped flour from a sack into a brown paper bag, and wrapped a chunk of salt meat in an old newspaper. On going out to the sundowner, anger surged in him at the sight of the man standing by the bunk and looking through his mystery story.

"He, he! Detective yarn!" said the sundowner. "I give 'em away years ago. A bloke does a killing and leaves the clues for the detectives to find. They're all the same. Why in 'ell don't a bloke write about a bloke who kills another bloke and gets away with it? I could kill a bloke and leave no clues."

"You could," sneered Larkin.

"Course. Easy. You only gotta use your brain – like me."

Larkin handed over the rations and edged the visitor off his verandah. The fellow was batty, all right, but harmless as they all are.

"How would you kill a man and leave no clues?" he asked.

"Well, I tell you it's easy." The derelict pushed the rations into a dirty gunny sack and again sat down on his swag. "You see, mate, it's this way. In real life the murderer can't do away with the body. Even doctors and things like that make a hell of a mess of doing away with a corpse. In fact, they don't do away with it, mate. They leave parts and bits of it all over the scenery, and then what happens? Why, a detective comes along and he says, 'Cripes, someone's been and done a murder! Ah! Watch me track the bloke what done it.' If you're gonna commit a murder, you must be able to do away with the body. Having done that, well, who's gonna prove anything? Tell me that, mate."

"You tell me," urged Larkin, and tossed his depleted tobacco plug to the visitor. The sundowner gnawed from the plug, almost hit a dog in the eye with a spit, gulped, and settled to the details of the perfect murder.

"Well, mate, it's like this. Once you done away with the body, complete, there ain't nothing left to say that the body ever was alive to be killed. Now, supposin' I wanted to do you in. I don't, mate, don't think that, but I 'as plenty of time to work things out. Supposin' I wanted to do you in. Well, me and you is out ridin' and I takes me chance and shoots you stone-dead. I chooses to do the killin' where there's plenty of dead wood. Then I gathers the dead wood and drags your body onto it and fires the wood. Next day, when the ashes are cold, I goes back with a sieve and dolly pot. That's all I wants then.

"I takes out your burned bones and I crushes 'em to dust in the dolly pot. Then I goes through the ashes with the sieve, getting out all the small bones and putting them through the dolly pot. The dust I empties out from the dolly pot for the wind to take. All the metal bits, such as buttons and boot sprigs, I puts in me pocket and carries back to the homestead where I throws 'em down the well or covers 'em with sulphuric acid.

"Almost sure to be a dolly pot here, by the look of the place. Almost sure to be a sieve. Almost sure to be a jar of sulphuric acid for solderin' work. Everythin' on tap, like. And just in case the million-to-one chance comes off that someone might come across the fire site and wonder, sort of, I'd shoot a coupler kangaroos, skin 'em, and burn the carcasses on top of the old ashes. You know, to keep the blowies from breeding."

Harry Larkin looked at the sundowner, and through him. A prospector's dolly pot, a sieve, a quantity of sulphuric acid to dissolve the metal parts. Yes, they were all here. Given time a man could commit the perfect murder. Time! Two days would be long enough.

The sundowner stood up. "Good day, mate. Don't mind me. He, he! Flamin' hot, ain't it? Be cool down south. Well, I'll be movin."

Larkin watched him depart. The bush waif did not stop at the shed to camp for the night. He went on to the windmill and sprawled over the drinking trough to drink. He filled his rusty billy-can, Larkin watching until the mirage to the southward drowned him.

The perfect murder, with aids as common as household remedies. The perfect scene, this land without limits where even a man and his nearest neighbor are separated by nine miles. A prospector's dolly pot, a sieve, and a pint of soldering acid. Simple! It was as simple as being kicked to death in a stockyard jammed with mules.

"William Reynolds vanished three months ago, and repeated searches have failed to find even his body."

Mounted Constable Evans sat stiffly erect in the chair behind the littered desk in the Police Station at Wondong. Opposite him lounged a slight dark-complexioned man having a straight nose, a high forehead, and intensely blue eyes. There was no doubt that Evans was a policeman. None would guess that the dark man with the blue eyes was Detective Inspector Napoleon Bonaparte.

"The man's relatives have been bothering Headquarters about William Reynolds, which is why I am here," explained Bonaparte, faintly apologetic. "I have read your reports, and find them clear and concise. There is no doubt in the Official Mind that, assisted by your black tracker, you have done everything possible to locate Reynolds or his dead body. I may succeed where you and the black tracker failed because I am peculiarly equipped with gifts bequeathed to me by my white father and my aboriginal mother. In me are combined the white man's reasoning powers and the black man's perceptions and bushcraft. Therefore, should I succeed there would be no reflection on your efficiency or the powers of your tracker. Between what a tracker sees and what you have been trained to reason, there is a bridge. There is no such bridge between those divided powers in me. Which is why I never fail."

Having put Constable Evans in a more cooperative frame of mind, Bony rolled a cigarette and relaxed.

"Thank you, sir," Evans said and rose to accompany Bony to the locality map which hung on the wall. "Here's the township of Wondong. Here is the homestead of Morley Downs cattle station. And here, fifteen miles on from the homestead, is the stockman's hut where William Reynolds lived and worked.

"There's no telephonic communication between the hut and the homestead. Once every month the people at the homestead trucked rations to Reynolds. And once every week, every Monday morning, a stockman from the homestead would meet Reynolds midway between homestead and hut to give Reynolds his mail, and orders, and have a yarn with him over a billy of tea."

"And then one Monday, Reynolds didn't turn up," Bony added, as they resumed their chairs at the desk.

"That Monday the homestead man waited four hours for Reynolds," continued Evans. "The following day the station manager ran out in his car to Reynolds' hut. He found the ashes on the open hearth stone-cold, the two chained dogs nearly dead of thirst, and that Reynolds hadn't been at the hut since the day it had rained, three days previously.

"The manager drove back to the homestead and organised all his men in a search party. They found Reynolds' horse running with several others. The horse was still saddled and bridled. They rode the country for two days, and then I went out with my tracker to join in. We kept up the search for a week, and the tracker's opinion was that Reynolds might have been riding the back boundary fence when he was parted from the horse. Beyond that the tracker was vague, and I don't wonder at it for two reasons. One, the rain had wiped out tracks visible to white eyes, and two, there were other horses in the same paddock. Horse tracks swamped with rain are indistinguishable one from another."

"How large is that paddock?" asked Bony.

"Approximately 200 square miles."

Bony rose and again studied the wall map. "On the far side of the fence is this place named Reefer's Find," he pointed out. "Assuming that Reynolds had been thrown from his horse and injured, might he not have tried to reach the outstation of Reefer's Find which, I see, is about three miles from the fence whereas Reynolds' hut is six or seven?"

"We thought of that possibility, and we scoured the country on the Reefer's Find side of the boundary fence," Evans replied. "There's a stockman named Larkin at the Reefer's Find outstation. He joined in the search. The tracker, who had memorised Reynolds' footprints, found on the earth floor of the hut's verandah, couldn't spot any of his tracks on Reefer's Find country, and the boundary fence, of course, did not permit Reynolds' horse into that country. The blasted rain beat the tracker. It beat all of us."

"Him. Did you know this Reynolds?"

"Yes. He came to town twice on a bit of a bender. Good type. Good horseman. Good bushman. The horse he rode that day was not a tricky animal. What do Headquarters know of him, sir?"

"Only that he never failed to write regularly to his mother, and that he had spent four years in the Army from which he was discharged following a head wound."

"Head wound! He might have suffered from amnesia. He could have left his horse and walked away – anywhere – walked until he dropped and died from thirst or starvation."

"It's possible. What is the character of the man Larkin?"

"Average, I think. He told me that he and Reynolds had met when both happened to be riding that boundary fence, the last time being several months before Reynolds vanished."

"How many people besides Larkin at that outstation?"

"No one else excepting when they're mustering for fats."

The conversation waned while Bony rolled another cigarette. "Could you run me out to Morley Downs homestead?" he asked.

"Yes, of course," assented Evans.

"Then kindly telephone the manager and let me talk to him."

Two hundred square miles is a fairly large tract of country in which to find clues leading to the fate of a lost man, and three months is an appreciable period of time to elapse after a man is reported as lost.

The rider who replaced Reynolds' successor was blue-eyed and dark-skinned, and at the end of two weeks of incessant reading he was familiar with every acre, and had read every word on this large page of the Book of the Bush.

By now Bony was convinced that Reynolds hadn't died in that paddock. Lost or injured men had crept into a hollow log to die, their remains found many years afterward, but in this country there were no trees large enough for a man to crawl into. Men had perished and their bodies had been covered with wind-blown sand, and after many years the wind had removed the sand to reveal the skeleton. In Reynolds' case the search for him had been begun within a week of his disappearance, when eleven men plus a policeman selected for his job because of his bushcraft, and a black tracker selected from among the aborigines who are the best sleuths in the world, had gone over and over the 200 square miles.

Bony knew that, of the searchers, the black tracker would be the most proficient. He knew, too, just how the mind of that aborigine would work when taken to the stockman's hut and put on the job. Firstly, he would see the lost man's horse and memorize its hoofprints. Then he would memorize the lost man's bootprints left on the dry earth beneath the verandah roof. Thereafter he would ride crouched forward above his horse's mane and keep his eyes directed to the ground at a point a few feet beyond the animal's nose. He would look for a horse's tracks and a man's tracks, knowing that nothing passes over the ground without leaving evidence, and that even half an inch of rain will not always obliterate the evidence left, perhaps, in the shelter of a tree.

That was all the black tracker could be expected to do. He would not reason that the lost man might have climbed a tree and there cut his own throat, or that he might have wanted to vanish and so had climbed over one of the fences into the adjacent paddock, or had, when suffering from amnesia, or the madness brought about by solitude, walked away beyond the rim of the earth.

The first clue found by Bonaparte was a wisp of wool dyed brown. It was caught by a barb of the top wire of the division fence between the two cattle stations. It was about an inch in length and might well have come from a man's sock when he had climbed over the fence.

It was most unlikely that any one of the searchers for William Reynolds would have climbed the fence. They were all mounted, and when they scoured the neighbouring country, they would have passed through the gate about a mile from this tiny piece of flotsam. Whether or not the wisp of wool had been detached from Reynolds' sock at the time of his disappearance, its importance in this case was that it led the investigator to the second clue.

The vital attribute shared by the aboriginal tracker with Napoleon Bonaparte was patience. To both, Time was of no consequence once they set out on the hunt.

On the twenty-ninth day of his investigation Bony came on the site of a large fire. It was approximately a mile distant from the outstation of Reefer's Find, and, from a point nearby, the buildings could be seen magnified and distorted by the mirage. The fire had burned after the last rainfall – the one recorded immediately following the disappearance of Reynolds – and the trails made by dead tree branches when dragged together still remained sharp on the ground.

The obvious purpose of the fire had been to consume the carcass of a calf, for amid the mound of white ash protruded the skull and bones of the animal. The wind had played with the ash, scattering it thinly all about the original ash mound.

Question: "Why had Larkin burned the carcass of the calf?" Cattlemen never do such a thing unless a beast dies close to their camp. In parts of the continent, carcasses are always burned to keep down the blowfly pest, but out here in the interior, never. There was a possible answer, however, in the mentality of the man who lived nearby, the man who lived alone and could be expected to do anything unusual, even burning all the carcasses of animals which perished in his domain. That answer would be proved correct if other fire sites were discovered offering the same evidence.

At daybreak the next morning Bony was perched high in a sandalwood tree. There he watched Larkin ride out on his day's work, and when assured that the man was out of the way, he slid to the ground and examined the ashes and the burned bones, using his hands and his fingers as a sieve.

Other than the bones of the calf, he found nothing but a soft nosed bullet. Under the ashes, near the edge of the splayed-out mass, he found an indentation on the ground, circular and about six inches in diameter. The bullet and the mark were the second and third clues, the third being the imprint of a prospector's dolly pot.

"Do your men shoot calves in the paddocks for any reason?" Bony asked the manager, who had driven out to his hut with rations. The manager was big and tough, grizzled and shrewd.

"No, of course not, unless a calf has been injured in some way and is helpless. Have you found any of our calves shot?"

"None of yours. How do your stockmen obtain their meat supply?"

"We kill at the homestead and distribute fortnightly a little fresh meat and a quantity of salted beef."

"D'you think the man over on Reefer's Find would be similarly supplied by his employer?"

"Yes, I think so. I could find out from the owner of Reefer's Find."

"Please do. You have been most helpful, and I do appreciate it. In my role of cattleman it wouldn't do to have another rider stationed with me, and I would be grateful if you consented to drive out here in the evening for the next three days. Should I not be here, then wait until eight o'clock before taking from the tea tin over there on the shelf a sealed envelope addressed to you. Act on the enclosed instructions."

"Very well, I'll do that."

"Thanks. Would you care to undertake a little inquiry for me?"

"Certainly."

"Then talk guardedly to those men you sent to meet Reynolds every Monday and ascertain from them the relationship which existed between Reynolds and Harry Larkin. As is often the case with lonely men stationed near the boundary fence of two properties, according to Larkin he and Reynolds used to meet now and then by arrangement. They may have quarrelled. Have you ever met Larkin?"

"On several occasions, yes," replied the manager.

"And your impressions of him? As a man?"

"I thought him intelligent. Inclined to be morose, of course, but then men who live alone often are. You are not thinking that –?"

"I'm thinking that Reynolds is not in your country. Had he been still on your property, I would have found him dead or alive. When I set out to find a missing man, I find him. I shall find Reynolds, eventually – if there is anything of him to find."

On the third evening that the manager went out to the little hut, Bony showed him a small and slightly convex disk of silver. It was weathered and in one place cracked. It bore the initials JMM.

"I found that in the vicinity of the site of a large fire," Bony said. "It might establish that William Reynolds is no longer alive."

Although Harry Larkin was supremely confident, he was not quite happy. He had not acted without looking at the problem from all angles and without having earnestly sought the answer to the question: "If I shoot him dead, burn the body on a good fire, go through the ashes for the bones which I pound to dust in a dolly pot, and for the metal bits and pieces which I dissolve in sulphuric acid, how can I be caught?" The answer was plain.

He had carried through the sundowner's method of utterly destroying the body of the murder victim, and to avoid the million-to-one-chance of anyone coming across the ashes of the fire and being made suspicious, he had shot a calf as kangaroos were scarce.

Yes, he was confident, and confident that he was justified in being confident. Nothing remained of Bill Reynolds, damn him, save a little grayish dust which was floating around somewhere.

The slight unhappiness was caused by a strange visitation, signs of which he had first discovered when returning home from his work one afternoon. On the ground near the blacksmith's shop he found a strange set of boot tracks which were not older than two days. He followed these tracks backward to the house, and then forward until he lost them in the scrub.

Nothing in the house was touched, as far as he could see, and nothing had been taken from the blacksmith's shop, or interfered with. The dolly pot was still in the corner into which he had dropped it after its last employment, and the crowbar was still leaning against the anvil. On the shelf was the acid jar. There was no acid in it. He had used it to dissolve, partially, buttons and the metal band around a pipestem and boot sprigs. The residue of those metal objects he had dropped into a hole in a tree eleven miles away.

It was very strange. A normal visitor, finding the occupier away, would have left a note at the house. Had the visitor been black, he would not have left any tracks if bent on mischief.

The next day Larkin rode out to the boundary fence and on the way he visited the site of his fire. There he found the plain evidence that someone had moved the bones of the animal and had delved among the ashes still remaining from the action of the wind.

Thus he was not happy, but still supremely confident. They could not tack anything onto him. They couldn't even prove that Reynolds was dead. How could they when there was nothing of him left?

It was again Sunday, and Larkin was washing his clothes at the outside fire when the sound of horses' hoofs led him to see two men approaching. His lips vanished into a mere line, and his mind went over all the answers he would give if the police ever did call on him. One of the men he did not know. The other was Mounted Constable Evans.

They dismounted, anchoring their horses by merely dropping the reins to the ground. Larkin searched their faces and wondered who the slim half-caste with the singularly blue eyes was.

"Good day," Larkin greeted them.

"Good day, Larkin," replied Constable Evans, and appeared to give his trousers a hitch. His voice was affable, and Larkin was astonished when, after an abrupt and somewhat violent movement, he found himself handcuffed.

"Going to take you in for the murder of William Reynolds," Evans announced. "This is Detective Inspector Napoleon Bonaparte."

"You must be balmy – or I am," Larkin said.

Evans countered with: "You are. Come on over to the house. A car will be here in about half an hour."

The three men entered the kitchen where Larkin was told to sit down.

"I haven't done anything to Reynolds, or anyone else," asserted Larkin, and for the first time the slight man with the brilliant blue eyes spoke.

"While we are waiting, I'll tell you all about it, Larkin. I'll tell it so clearly that you will believe I was watching you all the time. You used to meet Reynolds at the boundary fence gate, and the two of you would indulge in a spot of gambling – generally at poker. Then one day you cheated and there was a fight in which you were thrashed.

"You knew what day of the week Reynolds would ride that

boundary fence and you waited for him on your side. You held him up and made him climb over the fence while you covered him with your .32 high-power Savage rifle. You made him walk to a place within a mile of here, where there was plenty of dry wood, and there you shot him and burned his body.

"The next day you returned with a dolly pot and a sieve. You put all the bones through the dolly pot, and then you sieved all the ashes for metal objects in Reynolds' clothes and burned them up with sulphuric acid. Very neat. The perfect crime, you must agree."

"If I done all that, which I didn't, yes," Larkin did agree.

"Well, assuming that not you but another did all I have outlined, why did the murderer shoot and burn the carcass of a calf on the same fire site?"

"You tell me," said Larkin.

"Good. I'll even do that. You shot Reynolds and you disposed of his body, as I've related. Having killed him, you immediately dragged wood together and burned the body, keeping the fire going for several hours. Now, the next day, or the day after that, it rained, and that rainfall fixed your actions like words printed in a book. You went through the ashes for Reynolds' bones before it rained, and you shot the calf and lit the second fire after it rained. You dropped the calf at least 200 yards from the scene of the murder, and you carried the carcass on your back over those 200 yards. The additional weight impressed your boot prints on the ground much deeper than when you walk about normally, and although the rain washed out many of your boot prints, it did not remove your prints made when carrying the dead calf. You didn't shoot the calf, eh?"

"No, of course I didn't,' came the sneering reply. 'I burned the carcass of a calf that died. I keep my camp clean. Enough blowflies about as it is."

"But you burned the calf's carcass a full mile away from your camp. However, you shot the calf, and you shot it to burn the carcass in order to prevent possible curiosity. You should have gone through the ashes after you burned the carcass of the calf and retrieved the bullet fired from your own rifle."

Bony smiled, and Larkin glared.

Constable Evans said: "Keep your hands on the table, Larkin."

"You know, Larkin, you murderers often make me tired," Bony went on. "You think up a good idea, and then fall down executing it.

"You thought up a good one by dollying the bones and sieving the ashes for the metal objects on a man's clothes and in his boots, and then – why go and spoil it by shooting a calf and burning the carcass on the same fire site? It wasn't necessary. Having pounded Reynolds' bones to ash and scattered the ash to the four corners, and having retrieved from the ashes the remaining evidence that a human body had been destroyed, there was no necessity to burn a carcass. It wouldn't have mattered how suspicious anyone became. Your biggest mistake was burning that calf. That act connects you with that fire."

"Yes, well, what of it?" Larkin almost snarled. "I got a bit lonely livin' here alone for months, and one day I sorta got fed up. I seen the calf, and I up with me rifle and took a pot shot at it."

"It won't do," Bony said, shaking his head. "Having taken a pot shot at the calf, accidentally killing it, why take a dolly pot to the place where you burned the carcass? You did carry a dolly pot, the one in the blacksmith's shop, to the scene of the fire, for the imprint of the dolly pot on the ground is still plain in two places."

"Pretty good tale, I must say," said Larkin. "You still can't prove that Bill Reynolds is dead."

"No?" Bony's dark face registered a bland smile, but his eyes were like blue opals. "When I found a wisp of brown wool attached to the boundary fence, I was confident that Reynolds had climbed it, merely because I was sure his body was not on his side of the fence. You made him walk to the place where you shot him, and then you saw the calf and the other cattle in the distance, and you shot the calf and carried it to the fire.

"I have enough to put you in the dock, Larkin – and one other little thing which is going to make certain you'll hang. Reynolds was in the Army during the war. He was discharged following a head wound. The surgeon who operated on Reynolds was a specialist in trepanning. The surgeon always scratched his initials on the silver plate he inserted into the skull of a patient. He has it on record that he operated on William Reynolds, and he will swear that the plate came from the head of William Reynolds, and will also swear that the plate could not have been detached from Reynolds' head without great violence."

"It wasn't in the ashes," gasped Larkin, and then realized his slip.

"No, it wasn't in the ashes, Larkin," Bony agreed. "You see, when you shot him at close quarters, probably through the forehead, the expanding bullet took away a portion of the poor fellow's head – and the trepanning plate. I found the plate lodged in a sandalwood tree growing about thirty feet from where you burned the body."

Larkin glared across the table at Bony, his eyes freezing as he realised that the trap had indeed sprung on him.

Bony was again smiling. He said, as though comfortingly: "Don't fret, Larkin. If you had not made all those silly mistakes, you would have made others equally fatal. Strangely enough, the act of homicide always throws a man off balance. If it were not so, I would find life rather boring."

ACKNOWLEDGEMENTS

1 **A Tale of Bermagui** - First published in *Bermagui* magazine by BBGAC 1939

2 **The Fish that danced on its Tail** - First published in *The Scream of the Reel,* edited by Jack Pollard, Lansdowne 1966.

3 **Marlin, King of Gamefish** - First published by UNESCO, 1956.

4 **With his Majesty the Swordfish at Bermagui** - First published in the BBGAC Bulletin 1937-38.

5 **Big Game Fishing in Australia** - an unpublished manuscript courtesy of William Upfield.

6 **A Clue Among Fish** - Chapter 4 of *The Mystery of Swordfish Reef* (Angus & Robertson, Sydney 1939). The map on page 54 was also published in most editions of this book.

7 **A Wisp of Wool and Disk of Silver** - This Bony story was written in 1949 and sent to *Ellery Queen's Mystery Magazine* where it was mislaid, and finally published there in 1979.

Other Titles by Arthur W. Upfield and published by ETT Imprint:

Upfield's own drawing of Bony

Bony Novels by Upfield:

www.ingramcontent.com/pod-product-compliance
Lightning Source LLC
Chambersburg PA
CBHW051210090426

42740CB00021B/3443